C-161  CAREER EXAMINATION SERIES

*This is your*
*PASSBOOK for...*

# Computer Specialist

*Test Preparation Study Guide*
*Questions & Answers*

# COPYRIGHT NOTICE

This book is SOLELY intended for, is sold ONLY to, and its use is RESTRICTED to individual, bona fide applicants or candidates who qualify by virtue of having seriously filed applications for appropriate license, certificate, professional and/or promotional advancement, higher school matriculation, scholarship, or other legitimate requirements of education and/or governmental authorities.

This book is NOT intended for use, class instruction, tutoring, training, duplication, copying, reprinting, excerption, or adaptation, etc., by:

1) Other publishers
2) Proprietors and/or Instructors of "Coaching" and/or Preparatory Courses
3) Personnel and/or Training Divisions of commercial, industrial, and governmental organizations
4) Schools, colleges, or universities and/or their departments and staffs, including teachers and other personnel
5) Testing Agencies or Bureaus
6) Study groups which seek by the purchase of a single volume to copy and/or duplicate and/or adapt this material for use by the group as a whole without having purchased individual volumes for each of the members of the group
7) Et al.

Such persons would be in violation of appropriate Federal and State statutes.

PROVISION OF LICENSING AGREEMENTS – Recognized educational, commercial, industrial, and governmental institutions and organizations, and others legitimately engaged in educational pursuits, including training, testing, and measurement activities, may address request for a licensing agreement to the copyright owners, who will determine whether, and under what conditions, including fees and charges, the materials in this book may be used them.  In other words, a licensing facility exists for the legitimate use of the material in this book on other than an individual basis.  However, it is asseverated and affirmed here that the material in this book CANNOT be used without the receipt of the express permission of such a licensing agreement from the Publishers. Inquiries re licensing should be addressed to the company, attention rights and permissions department.

All rights reserved, including the right of reproduction in whole or in part, in any form or by any means, electronic or mechanical, including photocopying, recording, or by any information storage and retrieval system, without permission in writing from the Publisher.

Copyright © 2024 by
## National Learning Corporation

212 Michael Drive, Syosset, NY 11791
(516) 921-8888 • www.passbooks.com
E-mail: info@passbooks.com

PUBLISHED IN THE UNITED STATES OF AMERICA

# PASSBOOK® SERIES

THE *PASSBOOK® SERIES* has been created to prepare applicants and candidates for the ultimate academic battlefield – the examination room.

At some time in our lives, each and every one of us may be required to take an examination – for validation, matriculation, admission, qualification, registration, certification, or licensure.

Based on the assumption that every applicant or candidate has met the basic formal educational standards, has taken the required number of courses, and read the necessary texts, the *PASSBOOK® SERIES* furnishes the one special preparation which may assure passing with confidence, instead of failing with insecurity. Examination questions – together with answers – are furnished as the basic vehicle for study so that the mysteries of the examination and its compounding difficulties may be eliminated or diminished by a sure method.

This book is meant to help you pass your examination provided that you qualify and are serious in your objective.

The entire field is reviewed through the huge store of content information which is succinctly presented through a provocative and challenging approach – the question-and-answer method.

A climate of success is established by furnishing the correct answers at the end of each test.

You soon learn to recognize types of questions, forms of questions, and patterns of questioning. You may even begin to anticipate expected outcomes.

You perceive that many questions are repeated or adapted so that you can gain acute insights, which may enable you to score many sure points.

You learn how to confront new questions, or types of questions, and to attack them confidently and work out the correct answers.

You note objectives and emphases, and recognize pitfalls and dangers, so that you may make positive educational adjustments.

Moreover, you are kept fully informed in relation to new concepts, methods, practices, and directions in the field.

You discover that you are actually taking the examination all the time: you are preparing for the examination by "taking" an examination, not by reading extraneous and/or supererogatory textbooks.

In short, this PASSBOOK®, used directedly, should be an important factor in helping you to pass your test.

# COMPUTER SPECIALIST

## DUTIES
The work involves responsibility for performing a variety of computer operations and technical services. The incumbent routinely queries a database and uses a variety of computer software to prepare required and necessary reports, correspondence, and public relations material. The incumbent also ensures the efficient operation of a local area network including computer hardware, software and peripheral equipment. In addition, the incumbent performs help-desk and user-support related activities. Does related work as required.

## SCOPE OF EXAMINATION

1. **FUNDAMENTALS OF MICROCOMPUTER SYSTEMS.**
   These questions test for knowledge of basic concepts and terminology related to microcomputers. They cover such topics as microcomputer and peripheral equipment; storage media; types of software used with microcomputers; and other associated terms and concepts.

2. **USE AND OPERATION OF MICROCOMPUTERS AND RELATED PERIPHERAL EQUIPMENT.**
   These questions are designed to test for technical knowledge and concepts relevant to the operation of a microcomputer and associated peripheral equipment for word processing, spreadsheet analysis, data base management, data communications and other applications. The questions asked are not specific to any vendor or any model of microcomputer.

3. **PRINCIPLES OF PROVIDING USER SUPPORT.**
   These questions test for knowledge and skill in working in a user support situation. They cover such subjects as how to communicate effectively with users requesting help; how to deal with different types of situations; troubleshooting techniques; and how to gather, organize and make available technical information needed to provide support.

4. **TRAINING USERS OF COMPUTERS.**
   These questions test for knowledge of techniques for using computers arid approaches to training others to use them. They cover such subjects as use of computer hardware, software and applications; preparing and evaluating instruction materials; determining the level of trainees' knowledge and the use of computers to provide instruction and feedback. The questions on training depend upon good judgment and practical experience rather than knowledge of abstract principles.

# HOW TO TAKE A TEST

I. YOU MUST PASS AN EXAMINATION

*A. WHAT EVERY CANDIDATE SHOULD KNOW*

Examination applicants often ask us for help in preparing for the written test. What can I study in advance? What kinds of questions will be asked? How will the test be given? How will the papers be graded?

As an applicant for a civil service examination, you may be wondering about some of these things. Our purpose here is to suggest effective methods of advance study and to describe civil service examinations.

Your chances for success on this examination can be increased if you know how to prepare. Those "pre-examination jitters" can be reduced if you know what to expect. You can even experience an adventure in good citizenship if you know why civil service exams are given.

*B. WHY ARE CIVIL SERVICE EXAMINATIONS GIVEN?*

Civil service examinations are important to you in two ways. As a citizen, you want public jobs filled by employees who know how to do their work. As a job seeker, you want a fair chance to compete for that job on an equal footing with other candidates. The best-known means of accomplishing this two-fold goal is the competitive examination.

Exams are widely publicized throughout the nation. They may be administered for jobs in federal, state, city, municipal, town or village governments or agencies.

Any citizen may apply, with some limitations, such as the age or residence of applicants. Your experience and education may be reviewed to see whether you meet the requirements for the particular examination. When these requirements exist, they are reasonable and applied consistently to all applicants. Thus, a competitive examination may cause you some uneasiness now, but it is your privilege and safeguard.

*C. HOW ARE CIVIL SERVICE EXAMS DEVELOPED?*

Examinations are carefully written by trained technicians who are specialists in the field known as "psychological measurement," in consultation with recognized authorities in the field of work that the test will cover. These experts recommend the subject matter areas or skills to be tested; only those knowledges or skills important to your success on the job are included. The most reliable books and source materials available are used as references. Together, the experts and technicians judge the difficulty level of the questions.

Test technicians know how to phrase questions so that the problem is clearly stated. Their ethics do not permit "trick" or "catch" questions. Questions may have been tried out on sample groups, or subjected to statistical analysis, to determine their usefulness.

Written tests are often used in combination with performance tests, ratings of training and experience, and oral interviews. All of these measures combine to form the best-known means of finding the right person for the right job.

## II. HOW TO PASS THE WRITTEN TEST

### A. NATURE OF THE EXAMINATION

To prepare intelligently for civil service examinations, you should know how they differ from school examinations you have taken. In school you were assigned certain definite pages to read or subjects to cover. The examination questions were quite detailed and usually emphasized memory. Civil service exams, on the other hand, try to discover your present ability to perform the duties of a position, plus your potentiality to learn these duties. In other words, a civil service exam attempts to predict how successful you will be. Questions cover such a broad area that they cannot be as minute and detailed as school exam questions.

In the public service similar kinds of work, or positions, are grouped together in one "class." This process is known as *position-classification*. All the positions in a class are paid according to the salary range for that class. One class title covers all of these positions, and they are all tested by the same examination.

### B. FOUR BASIC STEPS

**1) Study the announcement**

How, then, can you know what subjects to study? Our best answer is: "Learn as much as possible about the class of positions for which you've applied." The exam will test the knowledge, skills and abilities needed to do the work.

Your most valuable source of information about the position you want is the official exam announcement. This announcement lists the training and experience qualifications. Check these standards and apply only if you come reasonably close to meeting them.

The brief description of the position in the examination announcement offers some clues to the subjects which will be tested. Think about the job itself. Review the duties in your mind. Can you perform them, or are there some in which you are rusty? Fill in the blank spots in your preparation.

Many jurisdictions preview the written test in the exam announcement by including a section called "Knowledge and Abilities Required," "Scope of the Examination," or some similar heading. Here you will find out specifically what fields will be tested.

**2) Review your own background**

Once you learn in general what the position is all about, and what you need to know to do the work, ask yourself which subjects you already know fairly well and which need improvement. You may wonder whether to concentrate on improving your strong areas or on building some background in your fields of weakness. When the announcement has specified "some knowledge" or "considerable knowledge," or has used adjectives like "beginning principles of…" or "advanced … methods," you can get a clue as to the number and difficulty of questions to be asked in any given field. More questions, and hence broader coverage, would be included for those subjects which are more important in the work. Now weigh your strengths and weaknesses against the job requirements and prepare accordingly.

**3) Determine the level of the position**

Another way to tell how intensively you should prepare is to understand the level of the job for which you are applying. Is it the entering level? In other words, is this the position in which beginners in a field of work are hired? Or is it an intermediate or advanced level? Sometimes this is indicated by such words as "Junior" or "Senior" in the class title. Other jurisdictions use Roman numerals to designate the level – Clerk I, Clerk II, for example. The word "Supervisor" sometimes appears in the title. If the level is not indicated by the title, check the description of duties. Will you be working under very close supervision, or will you have responsibility for independent decisions in this work?

### 4) Choose appropriate study materials

Now that you know the subjects to be examined and the relative amount of each subject to be covered, you can choose suitable study materials. For beginning level jobs, or even advanced ones, if you have a pronounced weakness in some aspect of your training, read a modern, standard textbook in that field. Be sure it is up to date and has general coverage. Such books are normally available at your library, and the librarian will be glad to help you locate one. For entry-level positions, questions of appropriate difficulty are chosen – neither highly advanced questions, nor those too simple. Such questions require careful thought but not advanced training.

If the position for which you are applying is technical or advanced, you will read more advanced, specialized material. If you are already familiar with the basic principles of your field, elementary textbooks would waste your time. Concentrate on advanced textbooks and technical periodicals. Think through the concepts and review difficult problems in your field.

These are all general sources. You can get more ideas on your own initiative, following these leads. For example, training manuals and publications of the government agency which employs workers in your field can be useful, particularly for technical and professional positions. A letter or visit to the government department involved may result in more specific study suggestions, and certainly will provide you with a more definite idea of the exact nature of the position you are seeking.

## III. KINDS OF TESTS

Tests are used for purposes other than measuring knowledge and ability to perform specified duties. For some positions, it is equally important to test ability to make adjustments to new situations or to profit from training. In others, basic mental abilities not dependent on information are essential. Questions which test these things may not appear as pertinent to the duties of the position as those which test for knowledge and information. Yet they are often highly important parts of a fair examination. For very general questions, it is almost impossible to help you direct your study efforts. What we can do is to point out some of the more common of these general abilities needed in public service positions and describe some typical questions.

1) General information

Broad, general information has been found useful for predicting job success in some kinds of work. This is tested in a variety of ways, from vocabulary lists to questions about current events. Basic background in some field of work, such as sociology or economics, may be sampled in a group of questions. Often these are principles which have become familiar to most persons through exposure rather than through formal training. It is difficult to advise you how to study for these questions; being alert to the world around you is our best suggestion.

2) Verbal ability

An example of an ability needed in many positions is verbal or language ability. Verbal ability is, in brief, the ability to use and understand words. Vocabulary and grammar tests are typical measures of this ability. Reading comprehension or paragraph interpretation questions are common in many kinds of civil service tests. You are given a paragraph of written material and asked to find its central meaning.

3) Numerical ability
Number skills can be tested by the familiar arithmetic problem, by checking paired lists of numbers to see which are alike and which are different, or by interpreting charts and graphs. In the latter test, a graph may be printed in the test booklet which you are asked to use as the basis for answering questions.

4) Observation
A popular test for law-enforcement positions is the observation test. A picture is shown to you for several minutes, then taken away. Questions about the picture test your ability to observe both details and larger elements.

5) Following directions
In many positions in the public service, the employee must be able to carry out written instructions dependably and accurately. You may be given a chart with several columns, each column listing a variety of information. The questions require you to carry out directions involving the information given in the chart.

6) Skills and aptitudes
Performance tests effectively measure some manual skills and aptitudes. When the skill is one in which you are trained, such as typing or shorthand, you can practice. These tests are often very much like those given in business school or high school courses. For many of the other skills and aptitudes, however, no short-time preparation can be made. Skills and abilities natural to you or that you have developed throughout your lifetime are being tested.

Many of the general questions just described provide all the data needed to answer the questions and ask you to use your reasoning ability to find the answers. Your best preparation for these tests, as well as for tests of facts and ideas, is to be at your physical and mental best. You, no doubt, have your own methods of getting into an exam-taking mood and keeping "in shape." The next section lists some ideas on this subject.

## IV. KINDS OF QUESTIONS

Only rarely is the "essay" question, which you answer in narrative form, used in civil service tests. Civil service tests are usually of the short-answer type. Full instructions for answering these questions will be given to you at the examination. But in case this is your first experience with short-answer questions and separate answer sheets, here is what you need to know:

### 1) Multiple-choice Questions
Most popular of the short-answer questions is the "multiple choice" or "best answer" question. It can be used, for example, to test for factual knowledge, ability to solve problems or judgment in meeting situations found at work.

A multiple-choice question is normally one of three types—
- It can begin with an incomplete statement followed by several possible endings. You are to find the one ending which *best* completes the statement, although some of the others may not be entirely wrong.
- It can also be a complete statement in the form of a question which is answered by choosing one of the statements listed.

- It can be in the form of a problem – again you select the best answer.

Here is an example of a multiple-choice question with a discussion which should give you some clues as to the method for choosing the right answer:

When an employee has a complaint about his assignment, the action which will *best* help him overcome his difficulty is to
- A. discuss his difficulty with his coworkers
- B. take the problem to the head of the organization
- C. take the problem to the person who gave him the assignment
- D. say nothing to anyone about his complaint

In answering this question, you should study each of the choices to find which is best. Consider choice "A" – Certainly an employee may discuss his complaint with fellow employees, but no change or improvement can result, and the complaint remains unresolved. Choice "B" is a poor choice since the head of the organization probably does not know what assignment you have been given, and taking your problem to him is known as "going over the head" of the supervisor. The supervisor, or person who made the assignment, is the person who can clarify it or correct any injustice. Choice "C" is, therefore, correct. To say nothing, as in choice "D," is unwise. Supervisors have and interest in knowing the problems employees are facing, and the employee is seeking a solution to his problem.

## 2) True/False Questions

The "true/false" or "right/wrong" form of question is sometimes used. Here a complete statement is given. Your job is to decide whether the statement is right or wrong.

SAMPLE: A roaming cell-phone call to a nearby city costs less than a non-roaming call to a distant city.

This statement is wrong, or false, since roaming calls are more expensive.

This is not a complete list of all possible question forms, although most of the others are variations of these common types. You will always get complete directions for answering questions. Be sure you understand *how* to mark your answers – ask questions until you do.

## V. RECORDING YOUR ANSWERS

Computer terminals are used more and more today for many different kinds of exams.
For an examination with very few applicants, you may be told to record your answers in the test booklet itself. Separate answer sheets are much more common. If this separate answer sheet is to be scored by machine – and this is often the case – it is highly important that you mark your answers correctly in order to get credit.

An electronic scoring machine is often used in civil service offices because of the speed with which papers can be scored. Machine-scored answer sheets must be marked with a pencil, which will be given to you. This pencil has a high graphite content which responds to the electronic scoring machine. As a matter of fact, stray dots may register as answers, so do not let your pencil rest on the answer sheet while you are pondering the correct answer. Also, if your pencil lead breaks or is otherwise defective, ask for another.

Since the answer sheet will be dropped in a slot in the scoring machine, be careful not to bend the corners or get the paper crumpled.

The answer sheet normally has five vertical columns of numbers, with 30 numbers to a column. These numbers correspond to the question numbers in your test booklet. After each number, going across the page are four or five pairs of dotted lines. These short dotted lines have small letters or numbers above them. The first two pairs may also have a "T" or "F" above the letters. This indicates that the first two pairs only are to be used if the questions are of the true-false type. If the questions are multiple choice, disregard the "T" and "F" and pay attention only to the small letters or numbers.

Answer your questions in the manner of the sample that follows:

32. The largest city in the United States is
    A. Washington, D.C.
    B. New York City
    C. Chicago
    D. Detroit
    E. San Francisco

1) Choose the answer you think is best. (New York City is the largest, so "B" is correct.)
2) Find the row of dotted lines numbered the same as the question you are answering. (Find row number 32)
3) Find the pair of dotted lines corresponding to the answer. (Find the pair of lines under the mark "B.")
4) Make a solid black mark between the dotted lines.

## VI. BEFORE THE TEST

Common sense will help you find procedures to follow to get ready for an examination. Too many of us, however, overlook these sensible measures. Indeed, nervousness and fatigue have been found to be the most serious reasons why applicants fail to do their best on civil service tests. Here is a list of reminders:

- Begin your preparation early – Don't wait until the last minute to go scurrying around for books and materials or to find out what the position is all about.
- Prepare continuously – An hour a night for a week is better than an all-night cram session. This has been definitely established. What is more, a night a week for a month will return better dividends than crowding your study into a shorter period of time.
- Locate the place of the exam – You have been sent a notice telling you when and where to report for the examination. If the location is in a different town or otherwise unfamiliar to you, it would be well to inquire the best route and learn something about the building.
- Relax the night before the test – Allow your mind to rest. Do not study at all that night. Plan some mild recreation or diversion; then go to bed early and get a good night's sleep.
- Get up early enough to make a leisurely trip to the place for the test – This way unforeseen events, traffic snarls, unfamiliar buildings, etc. will not upset you.
- Dress comfortably – A written test is not a fashion show. You will be known by number and not by name, so wear something comfortable.

- Leave excess paraphernalia at home – Shopping bags and odd bundles will get in your way. You need bring only the items mentioned in the official notice you received; usually everything you need is provided. Do not bring reference books to the exam. They will only confuse those last minutes and be taken away from you when in the test room.
- Arrive somewhat ahead of time – If because of transportation schedules you must get there very early, bring a newspaper or magazine to take your mind off yourself while waiting.
- Locate the examination room – When you have found the proper room, you will be directed to the seat or part of the room where you will sit. Sometimes you are given a sheet of instructions to read while you are waiting. Do not fill out any forms until you are told to do so; just read them and be prepared.
- Relax and prepare to listen to the instructions
- If you have any physical problem that may keep you from doing your best, be sure to tell the test administrator. If you are sick or in poor health, you really cannot do your best on the exam. You can come back and take the test some other time.

VII. AT THE TEST

The day of the test is here and you have the test booklet in your hand. The temptation to get going is very strong. Caution! There is more to success than knowing the right answers. You must know how to identify your papers and understand variations in the type of short-answer question used in this particular examination. Follow these suggestions for maximum results from your efforts:

1) **Cooperate with the monitor**

The test administrator has a duty to create a situation in which you can be as much at ease as possible. He will give instructions, tell you when to begin, check to see that you are marking your answer sheet correctly, and so on. He is not there to guard you, although he will see that your competitors do not take unfair advantage. He wants to help you do your best.

2) **Listen to all instructions**

Don't jump the gun! Wait until you understand all directions. In most civil service tests you get more time than you need to answer the questions. So don't be in a hurry. Read each word of instructions until you clearly understand the meaning. Study the examples, listen to all announcements and follow directions. Ask questions if you do not understand what to do.

3) **Identify your papers**

Civil service exams are usually identified by number only. You will be assigned a number; you must not put your name on your test papers. Be sure to copy your number correctly. Since more than one exam may be given, copy your exact examination title.

4) **Plan your time**

Unless you are told that a test is a "speed" or "rate of work" test, speed itself is usually not important. Time enough to answer all the questions will be provided, but this does not mean that you have all day. An overall time limit has been set. Divide the total time (in minutes) by the number of questions to determine the approximate time you have for each question.

### 5) Do not linger over difficult questions

If you come across a difficult question, mark it with a paper clip (useful to have along) and come back to it when you have been through the booklet. One caution if you do this – be sure to skip a number on your answer sheet as well. Check often to be sure that you have not lost your place and that you are marking in the row numbered the same as the question you are answering.

### 6) Read the questions

Be sure you know what the question asks! Many capable people are unsuccessful because they failed to *read* the questions correctly.

### 7) Answer all questions

Unless you have been instructed that a penalty will be deducted for incorrect answers, it is better to guess than to omit a question.

### 8) Speed tests

It is often better NOT to guess on speed tests. It has been found that on timed tests people are tempted to spend the last few seconds before time is called in marking answers at random – without even reading them – in the hope of picking up a few extra points. To discourage this practice, the instructions may warn you that your score will be "corrected" for guessing. That is, a penalty will be applied. The incorrect answers will be deducted from the correct ones, or some other penalty formula will be used.

### 9) Review your answers

If you finish before time is called, go back to the questions you guessed or omitted to give them further thought. Review other answers if you have time.

### 10) Return your test materials

If you are ready to leave before others have finished or time is called, take ALL your materials to the monitor and leave quietly. Never take any test material with you. The monitor can discover whose papers are not complete, and taking a test booklet may be grounds for disqualification.

## VIII. EXAMINATION TECHNIQUES

1) Read the general instructions carefully. These are usually printed on the first page of the exam booklet. As a rule, these instructions refer to the timing of the examination; the fact that you should not start work until the signal and must stop work at a signal, etc. If there are any *special* instructions, such as a choice of questions to be answered, make sure that you note this instruction carefully.

2) When you are ready to start work on the examination, that is as soon as the signal has been given, read the instructions to each question booklet, underline any key words or phrases, such as *least, best, outline, describe* and the like. In this way you will tend to answer as requested rather than discover on reviewing your paper that you *listed without describing*, that you selected the *worst* choice rather than the *best* choice, etc.

3) If the examination is of the objective or multiple-choice type – that is, each question will also give a series of possible answers: A, B, C or D, and you are called upon to select the best answer and write the letter next to that answer on your answer paper – it is advisable to start answering each question in turn. There may be anywhere from 50 to 100 such questions in the three or four hours allotted and you can see how much time would be taken if you read through all the questions before beginning to answer any. Furthermore, if you come across a question or group of questions which you know would be difficult to answer, it would undoubtedly affect your handling of all the other questions.

4) If the examination is of the essay type and contains but a few questions, it is a moot point as to whether you should read all the questions before starting to answer any one. Of course, if you are given a choice – say five out of seven and the like – then it is essential to read all the questions so you can eliminate the two that are most difficult. If, however, you are asked to answer all the questions, there may be danger in trying to answer the easiest one first because you may find that you will spend too much time on it. The best technique is to answer the first question, then proceed to the second, etc.

5) Time your answers. Before the exam begins, write down the time it started, then add the time allowed for the examination and write down the time it must be completed, then divide the time available somewhat as follows:
   - If 3-1/2 hours are allowed, that would be 210 minutes. If you have 80 objective-type questions, that would be an average of 2-1/2 minutes per question. Allow yourself no more than 2 minutes per question, or a total of 160 minutes, which will permit about 50 minutes to review.
   - If for the time allotment of 210 minutes there are 7 essay questions to answer, that would average about 30 minutes a question. Give yourself only 25 minutes per question so that you have about 35 minutes to review.

6) The most important instruction is to *read each question* and make sure you know what is wanted. The second most important instruction is to *time yourself properly* so that you answer every question. The third most important instruction is to *answer every question*. Guess if you have to but include something for each question. Remember that you will receive no credit for a blank and will probably receive some credit if you write something in answer to an essay question. If you guess a letter – say "B" for a multiple-choice question – you may have guessed right. If you leave a blank as an answer to a multiple-choice question, the examiners may respect your feelings but it will not add a point to your score. Some exams may penalize you for wrong answers, so in such cases *only*, you may not want to guess unless you have some basis for your answer.

7) Suggestions
   a. Objective-type questions
      1. Examine the question booklet for proper sequence of pages and questions
      2. Read all instructions carefully
      3. Skip any question which seems too difficult; return to it after all other questions have been answered
      4. Apportion your time properly; do not spend too much time on any single question or group of questions

5. Note and underline key words – *all, most, fewest, least, best, worst, same, opposite,* etc.
6. Pay particular attention to negatives
7. Note unusual option, e.g., unduly long, short, complex, different or similar in content to the body of the question
8. Observe the use of "hedging" words – *probably, may, most likely,* etc.
9. Make sure that your answer is put next to the same number as the question
10. Do not second-guess unless you have good reason to believe the second answer is definitely more correct
11. Cross out original answer if you decide another answer is more accurate; do not erase until you are ready to hand your paper in
12. Answer all questions; guess unless instructed otherwise
13. Leave time for review

b. Essay questions
1. Read each question carefully
2. Determine exactly what is wanted. Underline key words or phrases.
3. Decide on outline or paragraph answer
4. Include many different points and elements unless asked to develop any one or two points or elements
5. Show impartiality by giving pros and cons unless directed to select one side only
6. Make and write down any assumptions you find necessary to answer the questions
7. Watch your English, grammar, punctuation and choice of words
8. Time your answers; don't crowd material

8) Answering the essay question

Most essay questions can be answered by framing the specific response around several key words or ideas. Here are a few such key words or ideas:

M's: manpower, materials, methods, money, management
P's: purpose, program, policy, plan, procedure, practice, problems, pitfalls, personnel, public relations
   a. Six basic steps in handling problems:
      1. Preliminary plan and background development
      2. Collect information, data and facts
      3. Analyze and interpret information, data and facts
      4. Analyze and develop solutions as well as make recommendations
      5. Prepare report and sell recommendations
      6. Install recommendations and follow up effectiveness

   b. Pitfalls to avoid
      1. *Taking things for granted* – A statement of the situation does not necessarily imply that each of the elements is necessarily true; for example, a complaint may be invalid and biased so that all that can be taken for granted is that a complaint has been registered

2. *Considering only one side of a situation* – Wherever possible, indicate several alternatives and then point out the reasons you selected the best one
3. *Failing to indicate follow up* – Whenever your answer indicates action on your part, make certain that you will take proper follow-up action to see how successful your recommendations, procedures or actions turn out to be
4. *Taking too long in answering any single question* – Remember to time your answers properly

## IX. AFTER THE TEST

Scoring procedures differ in detail among civil service jurisdictions although the general principles are the same. Whether the papers are hand-scored or graded by machine we have described, they are nearly always graded by number. That is, the person who marks the paper knows only the number – never the name – of the applicant. Not until all the papers have been graded will they be matched with names. If other tests, such as training and experience or oral interview ratings have been given, scores will be combined. Different parts of the examination usually have different weights. For example, the written test might count 60 percent of the final grade, and a rating of training and experience 40 percent. In many jurisdictions, veterans will have a certain number of points added to their grades.

After the final grade has been determined, the names are placed in grade order and an eligible list is established. There are various methods for resolving ties between those who get the same final grade – probably the most common is to place first the name of the person whose application was received first. Job offers are made from the eligible list in the order the names appear on it. You will be notified of your grade and your rank as soon as all these computations have been made. This will be done as rapidly as possible.

People who are found to meet the requirements in the announcement are called "eligibles." Their names are put on a list of eligible candidates. An eligible's chances of getting a job depend on how high he stands on this list and how fast agencies are filling jobs from the list.

When a job is to be filled from a list of eligibles, the agency asks for the names of people on the list of eligibles for that job. When the civil service commission receives this request, it sends to the agency the names of the three people highest on this list. Or, if the job to be filled has specialized requirements, the office sends the agency the names of the top three persons who meet these requirements from the general list.

The appointing officer makes a choice from among the three people whose names were sent to him. If the selected person accepts the appointment, the names of the others are put back on the list to be considered for future openings.

That is the rule in hiring from all kinds of eligible lists, whether they are for typist, carpenter, chemist, or something else. For every vacancy, the appointing officer has his choice of any one of the top three eligibles on the list. This explains why the person whose name is on top of the list sometimes does not get an appointment when some of the persons lower on the list do. If the appointing officer chooses the second or third eligible, the No. 1 eligible does not get a job at once, but stays on the list until he is appointed or the list is terminated.

# X. HOW TO PASS THE INTERVIEW TEST

The examination for which you applied requires an oral interview test. You have already taken the written test and you are now being called for the interview test – the final part of the formal examination.

You may think that it is not possible to prepare for an interview test and that there are no procedures to follow during an interview. Our purpose is to point out some things you can do in advance that will help you and some good rules to follow and pitfalls to avoid while you are being interviewed.

*What is an interview supposed to test?*

The written examination is designed to test the technical knowledge and competence of the candidate; the oral is designed to evaluate intangible qualities, not readily measured otherwise, and to establish a list showing the relative fitness of each candidate – as measured against his competitors – for the position sought. Scoring is not on the basis of "right" and "wrong," but on a sliding scale of values ranging from "not passable" to "outstanding." As a matter of fact, it is possible to achieve a relatively low score without a single "incorrect" answer because of evident weakness in the qualities being measured.

Occasionally, an examination may consist entirely of an oral test – either an individual or a group oral. In such cases, information is sought concerning the technical knowledges and abilities of the candidate, since there has been no written examination for this purpose. More commonly, however, an oral test is used to supplement a written examination.

*Who conducts interviews?*

The composition of oral boards varies among different jurisdictions. In nearly all, a representative of the personnel department serves as chairman. One of the members of the board may be a representative of the department in which the candidate would work. In some cases, "outside experts" are used, and, frequently, a businessman or some other representative of the general public is asked to serve. Labor and management or other special groups may be represented. The aim is to secure the services of experts in the appropriate field.

However the board is composed, it is a good idea (and not at all improper or unethical) to ascertain in advance of the interview who the members are and what groups they represent. When you are introduced to them, you will have some idea of their backgrounds and interests, and at least you will not stutter and stammer over their names.

*What should be done before the interview?*

While knowledge about the board members is useful and takes some of the surprise element out of the interview, there is other preparation which is more substantive. It *is* possible to prepare for an oral interview – in several ways:

**1) Keep a copy of your application and review it carefully before the interview**

This may be the only document before the oral board, and the starting point of the interview. Know what education and experience you have listed there, and the sequence and dates of all of it. Sometimes the board will ask you to review the highlights of your experience for them; you should not have to hem and haw doing it.

**2) Study the class specification and the examination announcement**

Usually, the oral board has one or both of these to guide them. The qualities, characteristics or knowledges required by the position sought are stated in these documents. They offer valuable clues as to the nature of the oral interview. For example, if the job involves supervisory responsibilities, the announcement will usually indicate that knowledge of modern supervisory methods and the qualifications of the candidate as a supervisor will be tested. If so, you can expect such questions, frequently in the form of a hypothetical situation which you are expected to solve. NEVER go into an oral without knowledge of the duties and responsibilities of the job you seek.

### 3) Think through each qualification required

Try to visualize the kind of questions you would ask if you were a board member. How well could you answer them? Try especially to appraise your own knowledge and background in each area, *measured against the job sought*, and identify any areas in which you are weak. Be critical and realistic – do not flatter yourself.

### 4) Do some general reading in areas in which you feel you may be weak

For example, if the job involves supervision and your past experience has NOT, some general reading in supervisory methods and practices, particularly in the field of human relations, might be useful. Do NOT study agency procedures or detailed manuals. The oral board will be testing your understanding and capacity, not your memory.

### 5) Get a good night's sleep and watch your general health and mental attitude

You will want a clear head at the interview. Take care of a cold or any other minor ailment, and of course, no hangovers.

*What should be done on the day of the interview?*

Now comes the day of the interview itself. Give yourself plenty of time to get there. Plan to arrive somewhat ahead of the scheduled time, particularly if your appointment is in the fore part of the day. If a previous candidate fails to appear, the board might be ready for you a bit early. By early afternoon an oral board is almost invariably behind schedule if there are many candidates, and you may have to wait. Take along a book or magazine to read, or your application to review, but leave any extraneous material in the waiting room when you go in for your interview. In any event, relax and compose yourself.

The matter of dress is important. The board is forming impressions about you – from your experience, your manners, your attitude, and your appearance. Give your personal appearance careful attention. Dress your best, but not your flashiest. Choose conservative, appropriate clothing, and be sure it is immaculate. This is a business interview, and your appearance should indicate that you regard it as such. Besides, being well groomed and properly dressed will help boost your confidence.

Sooner or later, someone will call your name and escort you into the interview room. *This is it.* From here on you are on your own. It is too late for any more preparation. But remember, you asked for this opportunity to prove your fitness, and you are here because your request was granted.

*What happens when you go in?*

The usual sequence of events will be as follows: The clerk (who is often the board stenographer) will introduce you to the chairman of the oral board, who will introduce you to the other members of the board. Acknowledge the introductions before you sit down. Do not be surprised if you find a microphone facing you or a stenotypist sitting by. Oral interviews are usually recorded in the event of an appeal or other review.

Usually the chairman of the board will open the interview by reviewing the highlights of your education and work experience from your application – primarily for the benefit of the other members of the board, as well as to get the material into the record. Do not interrupt or comment unless there is an error or significant misinterpretation; if that is the case, do not hesitate. But do not quibble about insignificant matters. Also, he will usually ask you some question about your education, experience or your present job – partly to get you to start talking and to establish the interviewing "rapport." He may start the actual questioning, or turn it over to one of the other members. Frequently, each member undertakes the questioning on a particular area, one in which he is perhaps most competent, so you can expect each member to participate in the examination. Because time is limited, you may also expect some rather abrupt switches in the direction the questioning takes, so do not be upset by it. Normally, a board member will not pursue a single line of questioning unless he discovers a particular strength or weakness.

After each member has participated, the chairman will usually ask whether any member has any further questions, then will ask you if you have anything you wish to add. Unless you are expecting this question, it may floor you. Worse, it may start you off on an extended, extemporaneous speech. The board is not usually seeking more information. The question is principally to offer you a last opportunity to present further qualifications or to indicate that you have nothing to add. So, if you feel that a significant qualification or characteristic has been overlooked, it is proper to point it out in a sentence or so. Do not compliment the board on the thoroughness of their examination – they have been sketchy, and you know it. If you wish, merely say, "No thank you, I have nothing further to add." This is a point where you can "talk yourself out" of a good impression or fail to present an important bit of information. Remember, *you close the interview yourself*.

The chairman will then say, "That is all, Mr. _____, thank you." Do not be startled; the interview is over, and quicker than you think. Thank him, gather your belongings and take your leave. Save your sigh of relief for the other side of the door.

*How to put your best foot forward*

Throughout this entire process, you may feel that the board individually and collectively is trying to pierce your defenses, seek out your hidden weaknesses and embarrass and confuse you. Actually, this is not true. They are obliged to make an appraisal of your qualifications for the job you are seeking, and they want to see you in your best light. Remember, they must interview all candidates and a non-cooperative candidate may become a failure in spite of their best efforts to bring out his qualifications. Here are 15 suggestions that will help you:

**1) Be natural – Keep your attitude confident, not cocky**

If you are not confident that you can do the job, do not expect the board to be. Do not apologize for your weaknesses, try to bring out your strong points. The board is interested in a positive, not negative, presentation. Cockiness will antagonize any board member and make him wonder if you are covering up a weakness by a false show of strength.

**2) Get comfortable, but don't lounge or sprawl**

Sit erectly but not stiffly. A careless posture may lead the board to conclude that you are careless in other things, or at least that you are not impressed by the importance of the occasion. Either conclusion is natural, even if incorrect. Do not fuss with your clothing, a pencil or an ashtray. Your hands may occasionally be useful to emphasize a point; do not let them become a point of distraction.

**3) Do not wisecrack or make small talk**

This is a serious situation, and your attitude should show that you consider it as such. Further, the time of the board is limited – they do not want to waste it, and neither should you.

**4) Do not exaggerate your experience or abilities**

In the first place, from information in the application or other interviews and sources, the board may know more about you than you think. Secondly, you probably will not get away with it. An experienced board is rather adept at spotting such a situation, so do not take the chance.

**5) If you know a board member, do not make a point of it, yet do not hide it**

Certainly you are not fooling him, and probably not the other members of the board. Do not try to take advantage of your acquaintanceship – it will probably do you little good.

**6) Do not dominate the interview**

Let the board do that. They will give you the clues – do not assume that you have to do all the talking. Realize that the board has a number of questions to ask you, and do not try to take up all the interview time by showing off your extensive knowledge of the answer to the first one.

**7) Be attentive**

You only have 20 minutes or so, and you should keep your attention at its sharpest throughout. When a member is addressing a problem or question to you, give him your undivided attention. Address your reply principally to him, but do not exclude the other board members.

**8) Do not interrupt**

A board member may be stating a problem for you to analyze. He will ask you a question when the time comes. Let him state the problem, and wait for the question.

**9) Make sure you understand the question**

Do not try to answer until you are sure what the question is. If it is not clear, restate it in your own words or ask the board member to clarify it for you. However, do not haggle about minor elements.

**10) Reply promptly but not hastily**

A common entry on oral board rating sheets is "candidate responded readily," or "candidate hesitated in replies." Respond as promptly and quickly as you can, but do not jump to a hasty, ill-considered answer.

**11) Do not be peremptory in your answers**

A brief answer is proper – but do not fire your answer back. That is a losing game from your point of view. The board member can probably ask questions much faster than you can answer them.

**12) Do not try to create the answer you think the board member wants**

He is interested in what kind of mind you have and how it works – not in playing games. Furthermore, he can usually spot this practice and will actually grade you down on it.

**13) Do not switch sides in your reply merely to agree with a board member**

Frequently, a member will take a contrary position merely to draw you out and to see if you are willing and able to defend your point of view. Do not start a debate, yet do not surrender a good position. If a position is worth taking, it is worth defending.

### 14) Do not be afraid to admit an error in judgment if you are shown to be wrong

The board knows that you are forced to reply without any opportunity for careful consideration. Your answer may be demonstrably wrong. If so, admit it and get on with the interview.

### 15) Do not dwell at length on your present job

The opening question may relate to your present assignment. Answer the question but do not go into an extended discussion. You are being examined for a *new* job, not your present one. As a matter of fact, try to phrase ALL your answers in terms of the job for which you are being examined.

*Basis of Rating*

Probably you will forget most of these "do's" and "don'ts" when you walk into the oral interview room. Even remembering them all will not ensure you a passing grade. Perhaps you did not have the qualifications in the first place. But remembering them will help you to put your best foot forward, without treading on the toes of the board members.

Rumor and popular opinion to the contrary notwithstanding, an oral board wants you to make the best appearance possible. They know you are under pressure – but they also want to see how you respond to it as a guide to what your reaction would be under the pressures of the job you seek. They will be influenced by the degree of poise you display, the personal traits you show and the manner in which you respond.

## ABOUT THIS BOOK

This book contains tests divided into Examination Sections. Go through each test, answering every question in the margin. We have also attached a sample answer sheet at the back of the book that can be removed and used. At the end of each test look at the answer key and check your answers. On the ones you got wrong, look at the right answer choice and learn. Do not fill in the answers first. Do not memorize the questions and answers, but understand the answer and principles involved. On your test, the questions will likely be different from the samples. Questions are changed and new ones added. If you understand these past questions you should have success with any changes that arise. Tests may consist of several types of questions. We have additional books on each subject should more study be advisable or necessary for you. Finally, the more you study, the better prepared you will be. This book is intended to be the last thing you study before you walk into the examination room. Prior study of relevant texts is also recommended. NLC publishes some of these in our Fundamental Series. Knowledge and good sense are important factors in passing your exam. Good luck also helps. So now study this Passbook, absorb the material contained within and take that knowledge into the examination. Then do your best to pass that exam.

# EXAMINATION SECTION

# EXAMINATION SECTION
# TEST 1

DIRECTIONS: Each question or incomplete statement is followed by several suggested answers or completions. Select the one that BEST answers the question or completes the statement. *PRINT THE LETTER OF THE CORRECT ANSWER IN THE SPACE AT THE RIGHT.*

1. Computer language is best described as a  1._____
   A. pattern  B. set of rules  C. sign  D. way to communicate

2. The _____ is the instructions for a computer to complete a task.  2._____
   A. function  B. statement  C. program  D. delimiter

3. The set of rules required to write a correct program is called  3._____
   A. instructions  B. semantics  C. syntax  D. language

4. Assembly language uses _____ to write code.  4._____
   A. mnemonics  B. binary 0s and 1s
   C. English  D. symbols

5. Which of the following data types is supported by a switch statement?  5._____
   A. Double  B. Float  C. Char  D. Boolean

6. Which is an invalid operator in Java?  6._____
   A. !  B. >?  C. ==  D. !=

7. ```
   public class Test{
       public static void main(String[]args){
       char a = 'a';
       int b = 97;
       String result = (a == b) ? "Equal" : "Not Equal";
       System.out.println(result);
       }
   }
   ```
   What is the output of the above code?  7._____
   A. Equal  B. Not Equal
   C. Compile-time error  D. Runtime error

8. Which one of the following data types is returned by (≥) relational operator?  8._____
   A. int  B. boolean  C. char  D. float

9. A class having two methods with the same name but different parameters is called  9._____
   A. Overloading  B. Overriding
   C. Hiding  D. Extending
   ```

10. Method Overloading is resolved at    10._____
    A. Calling time          B. Runtime
    C. JVM start             D. Compile-time

11. Which one of the following statements is TRUE when passing an argument by value?    11._____
    A. The argument's copy is passed to a method parameter.
    B. Initial argument's reference is passed to a method parameter.
    C. The argument's copy is passed to a method parameter and changes made on parameter effects the original argument.
    D. Initial argument's reference is passed to a method parameter and changes made on parameter effects the original argument.

12. _____ overloading is not supported in Java.    12._____
    A. Method     B. Operator     C. Variable     D. Constructor

13. _____ operator is used to initialize an array.    13._____
    A. Creat      B. Malloc       C. New          D. Init

14. Which of the following array utilizations is INCORRECT?    14._____
    A. int array{} = int [10]              B. int array [] = new int[10]
    C. int [] array = new int[10]          D. int array [] array = new int[10]

15. 
```
public class Array Test{
    public static void main(String args[]){
        int sequence[] = new int[10];
        for (int a = 0; a < 10; ++a) {
            a++;
            sequence[a] = a;
            System.out.print(sequence[a] + "");
        }
    }
}
```
What will be the output of the above program?    15._____
    A. 0 1 2 3 4 5 6 7 8 9         B. 1 2 3 4 5 6 7 8 9 10
    C. 0 2 4 6 8                   D. 1 3 5 7 9

16. An array is a(n) _____ in Java.    16._____
    A. object     B. primitive    C. value        D. constraint

17. The _____ defines multiple objects of the same type.    17._____
    A. new        B. interface    C. class        D. variable

18. The _____ is the real world entity having properties and actions.    18._____
    A. method     B. variable     C. aspect       D. object

19. The _____ is used to invoke an object.    19._____
    A. method     B. thread       C. constructor  D. destructor

20. How do you keep class from being instantiated?
    A. Add static final constructor
    B. Add non-argument constructor with protected modifier
    C. Mark constructor abstract
    D. Mark constructor private

    20.____

21. Which of the following packages contains classes and interfaces for IO operations?
    A. javax.io
    B. java,net
    C. java.socket
    D. java.io

    21.____

22. Which of the following is NOT true for File object usage?
    A. To rename the file
    B. To interact with the content of file
    C. To get the properties of file
    D. To delete the file

    22.____

23. The class used to write file content is called a
    A. Scanner
    B. System
    C. String
    D. PrintWriter

    23.____

24. The class used to read file content is called a
    A. String
    B. System
    C. Scanner
    D. PrintWriter

    24.____

25. When an array is passed as a method argument, the method receives the parameter as a(n)
    A. array reference
    B. array copy
    C. half array
    D. selected item of array

    25.____

## KEY (CORRECT ANSWERS)

| | | | |
|---|---|---|---|
| 1. | D | 11. | A |
| 2. | C | 12. | B |
| 3. | C | 13. | C |
| 4. | A | 14. | A |
| 5. | C | 15. | D |
| 6. | B | 16. | A |
| 7. | A | 17. | C |
| 8. | B | 18. | D |
| 9. | A | 19. | C |
| 10. | D | 20. | D |

| | |
|---|---|
| 21. | D |
| 22. | B |
| 23. | D |
| 24. | C |
| 25. | A |

# TEST 2

DIRECTIONS: Each question or incomplete statement is followed by several suggested answers or completions. Select the one that BEST answers the question or completes the statement. *PRINT THE LETTER OF THE CORRECT ANSWER IN THE SPACE AT THE RIGHT.*

1. What makes Java "Write Once, Run Anywhere"?　　　　　　　　　　　　　1._____
   A. Binary sequence　　　　　　B. Mnemonics
   C. CLR　　　　　　　　　　　　D. Bytecode

2. Java is platform independent.　　　　　　　　　　　　　　　　　　　　　2._____
   The above statement is
   A. true　　　　B. false　　　C. partially true　　D. unclear

3. An engine that interprets compiled code into machine level code is the　　3._____
   A. JRE　　　　B. JVM　　　　C. JDK　　　　D. JMS

4. The command used to get running JVM instance is　　　　　　　　　　　　4._____
   A. java　　　　B. jjvm　　　　C. javac　　　　D. run

5. The concept of programming in which execution flow is determined by　　　5._____
   parameter is called a
   A. loop　　　　　　　　　　　　B. sequence
   C. decision-making statements　D. assignments

6. 　　public static void main (String[]args){　　　　　　　　　　　　　　　　6._____
   　　　　int count = 0;
   　　　　do {
   　　　　　　count++;
   　　　　　　System.out.println("Hello world");
   　　　　　　++count;
   　　　　} while (count < 10);
   　　}
   }

   What will be the output of the above code?
   "Hello world" prints _____ times.
   A. 4　　　　　B. 11　　　　C. 8　　　　D. 9

7. Which one of the following allows uncountable execution paths?　　　　　7._____
   A. If else　　B. Switch　　C. For loop　　D. While loop

8. 　for(;;){ }　　　　　　　　　　　　　　　　　　　　　　　　　　　　　　8._____
   The above statement is
   A. true　　　　　　　　　　　　B. false
   C. a runtime error　　　　　　　D. a compile-time error

9. 
```
Class Test {
    int a;
    int b;

    void math(int a, int b) {
        a * = 2;
        b / + 2;
    }

    public static void main(String args []){

        Test test = new Test();
        int a = 10
        int b - 20;
        test.math(a , b);
        System.out.println(a + "-" + b);
    }
}
```
What will be the output of the above program?
A. 20 – 10    B. 10 – 20    C. 30 – 20    D. 10 - 30

10. 
```
class Test {
    int a;
    int b;

    Test(int a, int b){
        this.a = a;
        this.b = b;
    }

    void calculate(Test test){
        test.a * = 2;
        test.b / = 2;
    }

    public static void main(String args [] {
        Test test = new Test(10,20);
        test.calculate(test);
        System.out.println(test.a + "-" + test.b);
    }
}
```
What will be the output of the above program?
A. 20 – 10    B. 10 – 20    C. 30 – 20    D. 10 - 30

11. ```
    class Overloading Test {
        int x;
        int y;

        void add(int a){
            x = a + 1;
            add(a,x);
        }

        void add(int a, int b){
            x = a + 2;
        }

        public static void main(String args [] {
            Overloading Test test = new Overloading Test();
            test.add(6);
            System.out.println(test.x);
        }
    }
    ```
    What will be the output of the above program?
    A. 6　　　　　　B. 8　　　　　　C. 7　　　　　　D. 10

12. ```
    public class Overloading Test {
        int x;
        int y;

        void addInteger(int x){
            this.x = x + 1;
        }
        void addInteger(int x, int y){
            this.x = x * 2;
        }
        public static void main(String args[] {
            Overloading Test test - new Overloading Test();
            int x = 0;
            test.addInteger(6, 7);
            System.out.println(test.x);
        }
    }
    ```
    What will be the output of the above program?
    A. 9　　　　　　B. 8　　　　　　C. 10　　　　　D. 12

13. If an array is of size 10 like array[10], then how can the fourth element access?
    A. array[4]　　　B. array(4)　　　C. array[3]　　　D. array(3)

14. In Java, String is a(n)
    A. object　　　　B. literal　　　　C. class　　　　D. interface

15. ```
    public class Test {
        public static void main(String []args){
            String str = new String("Hello");
            if("Hello" == str){
                System.out.println("Equal Values");
            } else {
                System.out.println("Not Equal Values");
            }
        }
    }
    ```
    What will be the output of the above program?
    A. The program will be compiled and print "Equal Values"
    B. The program will be compiled and print "Not Equal Values"
    C. Runtime error: string literals cannot be compared with String object
    D. The program will be compiled with warning "Dead Code" on else block

    15.____

16. ```
    public class Test {
        public static void main(String []args){
            String str1 = new String("Hello");
            String str2 = new String("Hello");

            if(str1.equals(str2) ) {
                System.out.println("Equal Objects");
            } else {
                System.out.println("Not Equal Objects");
            }
        }
    }
    ```
    What will be the output of the above program?
    A. The program will be compiled and print "Equal Objects"
    B. The program will be compiled and print "Not Equal Objects"
    C. Runtime error: string literals cannot be compared with String object
    D. The program will be compiled with warning "Dead Code" on else block

    16.____

17. Java does not fully qualify object-oriented methodology due to
    A. global variables          B. constants
    C. loops                     D. primitive data types

    17.____

18. _____ is the process of hiding details of a program that is unnecessary for a user in a particular context.
    A. Encapsulation             B. Abstraction
    C. Information Hiding        D. Data Hiding

    18.____

19. _____ is the process of bundling different items (like fields and methods) into a single class.
    A. Encapsulation             B. Abstraction
    C. Information Hiding        D. Data Hiding

    19.____

20. _____ is an ability of a class to get the properties of another class and promote reusability.
    A. Inheritance  B. Composition
    C. Aggregation  D. Association

21. Which of the following methods is used to get the size of the file in bytes?
    A. Size()  B. FileLength()  C. GetBytes()  D. Length()

22. _____ method is called to remove files from disk.
    A. Remove()  B. RemoveTo()
    C. Delete()  D. DeletePermanently()

23. Java provides _____ overloaded constructors to create File object.
    A. 1  B. 2  C. 3  D. 4

24. _____ method returns an array of files and directories name in the given directory path.
    A. List()  B. ListFiles()
    C. ListFiles(filter fileFilter)  D. ListRoots

25. Suppose Beta is the child class of Alpha
    Alpha a = new Alpha();
    Beta b = a;
    Which of the following expressions evaluates to false?
    A. Beta instanceof Alpha  B. Beta instanceof Beta
    C. Alpha instanceof Beta  D. Alpha instanceof Alpha

## KEY (CORRECT ANSWERS)

| | | | |
|---|---|---|---|
| 1. | D | 11. | B |
| 2. | C | 12. | D |
| 3. | B | 13. | C |
| 4. | A | 14. | C |
| 5. | C | 15. | B |
| 6. | A | 16. | A |
| 7. | B | 17. | D |
| 8. | A | 18. | B |
| 9. | B | 19. | A |
| 10. | A | 20. | A |

21. D
22. C
23. D
24. A
25. C

# TEST 3

DIRECTIONS: Each question or incomplete statement is followed by several suggested answers or completions. Select the one that BEST answers the question or completes the statement. *PRINT THE LETTER OF THE CORRECT ANSWER IN THE SPACE AT THE RIGHT.*

1. _____ is the ability of the program to handle unexpected conditions. 1._____
    A. Simplicity  B. Robustness
    C. Multithreaded  D. Scalable

2. The syntax error is also called the _____ error. 2._____
    A. runtime  B. logical
    C. stack overflow  D. compile time

3. A type of error not detected by the compiler is the _____ error. 3._____
    A. runtime  B. logical
    C. stack overflow  D. compile time

4. What is the searching and fixing of bugs in a source code called? 4._____
    A. Inspection  B. Watching  C. Debugging  D. Repairing

5. What happens when the following line of code is executed: 5._____
   for(;;){ }?
    A. Unexpected behavior of program  B. System goes in infinite loop
    C. "//" prints infinite times  D. "//" prints one time

6. 
```
public class Test {
    public static void main(String []args){
    int i = 2;

    switch(i){
        case 1:
        System.out.println(1);
        break;
        case 2:
        System.out.println(2);
        break;
        case 2:
        System.out.println(2);
        break;
    }
    }
}
```
6._____

   What is the expected output of the above code?
    A. 22  B. 2
    C. Duplicate case error  D. Runtime error

7. To skip a particular iteration and leave the remaining code execution, which statement is used?  
   A. Continue    B. Break    C. Return    D. Exit

8. Which of the following loops is executed even if the initial condition is false?  
   A. For    B. Do-while    C. While    D. For each

9. Which one of these cases is INVALID for method overloading?  
   A. Methods have same data types, same sequence, and same number of parameters in parameter list.  
   B. Methods have different data types but same number of parameters.  
   C. Methods have different data types and different number of parameters.  
   D. Methods have same data types and different number of parameters.

10. What will happen when the main method is overloaded in class?  
    A. Runtime error    B. Method is overloaded  
    C. Exception throws    D. Compile-time error

11. 
```
class Test {
    int x;
    int y;

    Test(){
        // write something here
    }
    Test(int x, int y){
        // write something here
    }
    Test(int x){
        // write something here
    }
}
```
In reading the above class, what do you understand by the constructors?  
   A. It is invalid to define multiple constructors.  
   B. Constructors must be in sequence with respect to the number of parameters.  
   C. They are overloaded constructors.  
   D. Default constructor must be private.

12. The _____ defines what object, method, and variable is visible in other parts of the program.  
    A. scope    B. lifetime    C. modifiers    D. state

13. The _____ method is used to explicitly put a String object in string pool.  
    A. format()    B. ValueOf()    C. intern()    D. toPool()

14. The modification of immutable String object results in  14.____
    A. a new object
    B. overriding an existing object
    C. Appending an existing object
    D. Creating a new object and dereferencing the existing object

15. When String is created using string literal, it is created in the  15.____
    A. heap          B. stack          C. string pool     D. register

16. When this line will execute: "Hello".compareToIgnoreCase("hEllo")"), what will be the output?  16.____
    A. 1             B. 0              C. -1              D. -2

17. _____ is a way of writing general code that can work on multiple types.  17.____
    A. Inheritance   B. Composition   C. Aggregation    D. Polymorphism

18. Instance member marked with _____ cannot be inherited.  18.____
    A. protected     B. default       C. private        D. public

19. Which one of the following statements is invalid about "this"?  19.____
    A. It is used to invoke current class instance.
    B. It can be used to refer current class object.
    C. It can be used to call current class method and fields.
    D. It can also be used to call static members.

20. _____ keyword is used to call the immediate super class instance, method, and constructor.  20.____
    A. Super         B. This          C. SuperClass     D. Strictfp

21. Which of the following constructors is used to initialize an input object for file? Scanner sc = new  21.____
    A. Scanner(tmp.txt)              B. Scanner(new File("tmp.txt"))
    C. Scanner("tmp.txt")            D. Scanner(File("tmp.txt"))

22. ```
    class InputOutput {
        public static void main(String []args){
            Scanner sc = new Scanner(System.in);
            inti = sc.nextInt();
            System.out.println(i);
            sc.close();
        }
    }
    ```
    22.____

    What will be the possible output of the above program when the user enters '21L'?
    A. The code throws runtime exception "InputMismatchException".
    B. 2L, long value is converted into integer and prints 2.
    C. The compiler takes 2L as string and prints '2L'.
    D. The compiler takes 2L as string and skips 'L' prints 2.
    ```

23. 
```
class InputOutput {
    public static void main(String []args){
        Scanner sc = new Scanner(System.in);
        Double d1 = sc.nextDouble();
        String line = sc.nextLine();
        Double d2 = sc.nextDouble();
        System.out.println(d1 + " "+d2);
        sc.close();
    }
}
```
What will be the possible output of the above program when the user enters '2' then Press Enter Key then enter '3'?
   A. Program is compiled successfully and prints '2 3'.
   B. Program throws runtime error and cannot convert integer into double.
   C. Program is compiled successfully, and prints '2.0 3.0'.
   D. Program is compiled successfully, and prints '2.0\n3.0'.

24. Scanner class has the _____ method to read a single word.
   A. nextWord()              B. next()
   C. nextString()            D. next(String pattern)

25. PrintWriter does not support writing raw bytes on the stream. What is the alternative way of writing bytes?
   A. Use encoded byte stream        B. Use unencoded byte stream
   C. Use byte array                 D. Use byte wrapper class

## KEY (CORRECT ANSWERS)

| | | | |
|---|---|---|---|
| 1. | B | 11. | C |
| 2. | D | 12. | A |
| 3. | B | 13. | C |
| 4. | C | 14. | A |
| 5. | B | 15. | C |
| 6. | C | 16. | C |
| 7. | A | 17. | D |
| 8. | B | 18. | C |
| 9. | A | 19. | D |
| 10. | D | 20. | A |

| | |
|---|---|
| 21. | C |
| 22. | A |
| 23. | C |
| 24. | B |
| 25. | B |

# TEST 4

DIRECTIONS: Each question or incomplete statement is followed by several suggested answers or completions. Select the one that BEST answers the question or completes the statement. *PRINT THE LETTER OF THE CORRECT ANSWER IN THE SPACE AT THE RIGHT.*

1. _____ data type represents indivisible and atomic value.  1._____
   A. Object   B. Class   C. Primitive   D. Pointer

2. The data representation component of a data type determines how value is stored in terms of  2._____
   A. size of heap
   B. register representation
   C. data size and format
   D. data encoding

3. What is the difference between variables and constants?  3._____
   A. Nothing
   B. Constant identifier must be in uppercase
   C. A variable can change its value, whereas constant cannot
   D. A constant can change variable, whereas variable cannot

4. Suppose: inti = 17, j = 0.17;
   If the following line executes "System.out.println(i==j);", then what is the possible outcome?  4._____
   A. Compile-time error
   B. True
   C. Runtime error
   D. False

5. 
   ```
   public class Test {
       public static void main(String []args){
           int sum = 0;

           for (int a = 0, b = 0; a < 5 & b < 5; ++a, b = a + 1){
               sum ++a;
           }
           System.out.println(sum);
       }
   }
   ```
   What is the output of the above code?  5._____
   A. 6   B. 14
   C. 5   D. Compile-time error

6. Super class of Exception is  6._____
   A. Exception   B. Throwable
   C. RuntimeException   D. IOExce

7. Which block must execute whether exception comes or not?  7._____
   A. Start   B. Catch   C. Finally   D. Finalize

15

8. ```
   class Test{
       public static void main(String[]args){
           try{
               int a = 10/0;
               System.out.print("in try");
               return;
           }catch(Exception e){
               System.out.print("in catch");
               return;
           }finally{
               System.out.print("in finally");
               return;
           }
       }
   }
   ```
   What is the output of the above code?
   A. In try
   B. In try in catch
   C. In catch in finally
   D. In try in finally

9. The _____ method is used to display detailed exception messages.
   A. printStackTrace()
   B. getMessage()
   C. printExceptionMessage()
   D. getException()

10. ```
    void checkScope(){
        int a = 0;
        {
            a = 10;
            {
                a = 13;
                {
                    a b = a + 14;
                }
            }
            System.out.println(a);
        }
    }
    ```
    Considering the above method, what is the expected output of variable 'a'?
    A. 0
    B. Compile-time error
    C. 13
    D. Out of Scope Exception

11. ```
    void checkScope(){
        int a = 0;
        {
            int b = a + 14;
        }
        System.out.println(b);
    }
    ```
    Considering the above method, what is the expected output of variable 'b'?
    A. 14
    B. 014
    C. Compile-time error
    D. Runtime error
    ```

12. 
```
void checkScope(){
    int a = 1;
    {
        int b = a + 14;
    }
        int b = a + 14;
    }
    int b = 10;
    System.out.println(b);
}
```
Considering the above method, what will be the expected output?
   A. Compile-time error as b initialized 3 times
   B. Compile-time error as b initialized in both outer and inner scope
   C. Runtime error
   D. Successfully executed as the first two initialized in their own scope and third one initialized at the end

12.____

13. A _____ statement returns the control to the caller.
   A. return       B. break       C. continue       D. goto

13.____

14. Which of the following is the possible line of code to check string starts with "Good" if string is "Good Morning"?
   A. If (s.startsWith("Good"))
   B. If (s.indexOf("Good") == 1)
   C. If (s.charAt(1) == 'G' && s.charAt(2) == 'o' && s.charAt(3) == 'o' && s.charAt() == 'd'){
   D. If (s.substring(0,3).equals("Good"))

14.____

15. The _____ method is used to convert byte array into a string.
   A. toStringArray()           B. toArrayChar()
   C. toArrayString()           D. toCharArray()

15.____

16. Suppose String str = "Good", the method _____ returns a new string "Good".
   A. s.trim(s)                 B. String.trim(s)
   C. trim(s)                   D. s.trim()

16.____

17. Which one of the following statements is CORRECT?
   A. int a = new int(10);
   B. int[] c = {2, 4, 6, 8};
   C. char[] d = new char();
   D. char[] e = new char{'i', 'j', 'k', 'l'}[];

17.____

18. ```
    public class Test{
        int num;
        Test(int num){
            ____.num = num;
        }
    }
    ```
    Which of the following keywords fills in the blank in the above code?
    A. super    B. obj    C. new    D. this

19. ```
    class test{
        public static void main(String []args){
            Beta beta = new Beta();
        }
    }
    class alpha{
        int val = 7;

        public Alpha(){
        printRay();
        System.out.println("In Alpha");
        }
        public void printRay(){
        }
    }
    class beta extends Alpha{
        public Beta(){
        System.out.println("In Beta");
        }
        public void print Ray(){
        System.out.println("Beta Ray");
        }
    }
    ```
    What will be the output of the above code?
    A. First Beta class constructor called Alpha class's constructor and print "Beta Ray" by calling the overridden child method then print "In Alpha" and at last print "In Beta"
    B. First Alpha class constructor called and print "Beta Ray" by calling the overridden child method then print "In Alpha" and at last print "In Beta"
    C. The Alpha class constructor called overridden method and print "Alpha Ray"
    D. The Beta class constructor called and prints "In Beta"

20. ```
    public class Test{
        public static void main(String []args){
            Alpha alpha = new Alpha();
            alpha.printRay();
            Beta beta = new Beta();
            beta.printRay();
        }
    }
    public class Alpha{
        public void printRay(){
            System.out.println(getRay());
        }
        public String getRay(){
            return "Alpha";
        }
    }
    public class Beta extends Alpha{
        public String getRay(){
            return "Beta";
        }
    }
    ```
    What will be the output of the above code?
    A. Alpha Alpha
    B. Alpha Beta
    C. Beta Alpha
    D. Beta Beta

21. What will be the output of the following code, when Beta is the child class of Alpha?
    A. Compile-time error: mismatch type
    B. Alpha a – new Alpha();
    C. Compiled successfully, object b get the reference of object a
    D. Runtime error: mismatch type

22. What will happen when the following line executes and user presses Enter Key?
    A. String line – sc.nextLine();
    B. A blank string is stored in line, and the program is terminated
    C. Space is stored in line, and the program is terminated
    D. Compile-time error because nextLine() does not return anything
    E. Runtime error because nextLine() returns character

23. _____ is an inherited field in the PrintWriter class to synchronize operations on stream.
    A. Synchronized
    B. Sync
    C. Hold
    D. Lock
    ```

24. Which one of the following given constructors is used to initialize an output object for file?
    PrintWriter writer = new
    A. PrintWriter(tmp.txt);
    B. PrintWriter(new File("tmp.txt"));
    C. PrintWriter(new file("tmp.txt"));
    D. PrintWriter(file("tmp.txt"));

25. PrintWriter has a _____ method to clear the data in buffer.
    A. close()   B. flush()   C. clear()   D. closeflush()

## KEY (CORRECT ANSWERS)

1. C
2. C
3. C
4. D
5. A

6. B
7. C
8. C
9. B
10. C

11. C
12. D
13. A
14. A
15. D

16. D
17. B
18. D
19. A
20. B

21. A
22. B
23. D
24. B
25. B

# EXAMINATION SECTION
## TEST 1

DIRECTIONS: Each question or incomplete statement is followed by several suggested answers or completions. Select the one that BEST answers the question or completes the statement. *PRINT THE LETTER OF THE CORRECT ANSWER IN THE SPACE AT THE RIGHT.*

1. Users use _____ devices to send instructions to the computer.  1.____
   A. input          B. output
   C. memory unit    D. handlers

2. The _____ number system is used to perform arithmetic operations.  2.____
   A. hexadecimal   B. decimal    C. binary    D. octal

3. The CPU executes instructions in _____ cycle.  3.____
   A. save/run       B. do/destroy
   C. convert/run    D. fetch/execute

4. The register that holds the address of the currently executing instruction is  4.____
   A. program counter    B. processor register
   C. bus                D. instant register

5. A device that is capable of both input and output operations is a _____ device.  5.____
   A. storage    B. output    C. input    D. display

6. An If statement supports expression that evaluate to a(n) _____ data type.  6.____
   A. int    B. boolean    C. char    D. string

7. private void checkIf(){  7.____
       boolean x = false;           //Line 1
       if(x=true){                  //Line 2
           system,out.prinln("True");   //Line 3
       }else{
           System.out.println("False");
       }
   }
   What will be the output of the above code?
   A. Syntax error on Line 1    B. Syntax error on Line 2
   C. True                      D. False

8. A switch statement can evaluate integer data type which includes  8.____
   A. byte, int, long     B. short, int, byte
   C. long, int, short    D. char, long, int

9. 
```
private void checkSwitch(){
    int a = 2;
    switch (a){
        default:
            a++;
        case 1:
            ++a;
    }
    System.out.println(a);
}
```
What will be the output of the above code?
A. 3
B. 2
C. 4
D. Syntax error, as default block comes before case statement

9.____

10. In switch case, a _____ keyword is used to execute code when none of the cases match with switch condition.
A. default    B. break    C. continue    D. match

10.____

11. When an object variable passes into method, object _____ is passed.
A. copy    B. reference    C. value    D. type

11.____

12. The reference variable holds _____, which is the address of a specific object in the heap.
A. bits
B. string
C. hex code
D. stack pointer

12.____

13. When the object reference passes into a method, a _____ of an object reference is passed. Hence, both (caller and called method) refer to the same object on the heap.
A. value
B. original
C. copy
D. string representation

13.____

14. 
```
public class PassByValue Test{
    public static void main (String { [] args){
        int x = 2;

        PassByValueTest passByValue Test = new PassByValueTest();

        System.out.println("Before change(2) x = " + x);
        passByValueTest.change(x);
        System,out,println("After change(1) x = " + x);
    }
    void change(int num){
        num = num + 1;
        System.out.println("changed value = " + num);
    }
}
```

14.____

What will be the output of the above code?
A. Before change(2) x = 2
changed value = 3
After change(2) x = 3
B. Before change(2) x = 3
changed value = 2
After change(2) x = 2
C. Before change(2) x = 2
changed value = 2
After change(2) x = 3
D. Before change(2) x = 2
changed value = 3
After change(2) x = 2

15. ```
    public class PassByRefereneTest{
       int num;
       void modifyIt(int num){
          num = num + 200;
          System.out.println("num in modify as" + num);
       }
       public static void main (String [] args) {
       PassByRefereneTest passByRefereneTest = new PassByRefereneTest();
       System.out.println("num = " + 4);
       passByRefereneTest.num = 4;
       passByRefereneTest.modifyIt(passByRefereneTest.num);
       System.out.println("num after modifyIt is " + passByRefereneTest.num);
       }
    }
    ```
    15.____

    What will be the output of the above code?
    A. num = 4
       num in modify as 204
       num after modifyIt is 4
    B. num = 4
       num in modify as 204
       num after modifyIt is 204
    C. num = 4
       num in modifyIt is 204
       num after modifyIt is 204
    D. num = 4
       num in modify as 4
       num after modifyIt is 4

16. Which of the following is an invalid array declaration or initialization?   16.____
    A. int[] ar = new int[] {1,2,3,4,5};
    B. int[] ar = new int[5];
    C. int[5] a = {1,2,3,4,5}
    D. int[]b = {1,2,3,4,5};

17. ```
    public class ArrayTest{
        public static void main(String[] args){
        char[] letters = {65, 'A', 0101};
        System.out,println((letters[0] == letters[1]) + " " + (letters[0] = = [2]));
        }
    }
    ```
    17.____

    What will be the output of the above code?
    A. Compile time error
    B. true false
    C. false false
    D. true true

18. ```
    public class ArrayTest{
        public static void main(String[] args){
            int[][] ab = {{1,2}, {3,4,7}, {5,6}};
            System.out.println(ab.length + " " + ab[1].length);
        }
    }
    ```
    What will be the output of the above code?
    A. Compilation error
    B. Statement ab[1].length throws ArrayIndexOutOfBoundsException
    C. 3 2
    D. 3 3

    18.____

19. How can an array last index be accessed?
    A. array.length            B. array.length-1
    C. array.size              D. array.size-1

    19.____

20. On what index is array's first element found?
    A. 0        B. 1        C. -1        D. null

    20.____

21. A(n) _____ is a specification of an object.
    A. aspect    B. interface    C. class    D. enum

    21.____

22. A(n) _____ of an object is defined by its data.
    A. state     B. behavior     C. operation    D. mode

    22.____

23. Which one of the following statements is TRUE about encapsulation?
    A. It is a bundling of related data and behavior of an object
    B. It is a process in which data is protected and accessed only from get and set methods
    C. It is a process in which information irrelevant to the user is hidden
    D. It is a process that allows data to be directly accessed

    23.____

24. The benefit of the _____ method is that it applies additional conditions and formatting before setting data into variable.
    A. local     B. accessor     C. mutator     D. anonymous

    24.____

25. The process of hiding details that are irrelevant to the user in a specific context is called
    A. encapsulation    B. abstraction    C. inheritance    D. polymorphism

    25.____
    ```

## KEY (CORRECT ANSWERS)

| | | | |
|---|---|---|---|
| 1. | A | 11. | B |
| 2. | C | 12. | A |
| 3. | D | 13. | C |
| 4. | A | 14. | D |
| 5. | A | 15. | A |
| 6. | B | 16. | C |
| 7. | C | 17. | D |
| 8. | B | 18. | D |
| 9. | C | 19. | B |
| 10. | A | 20. | A |

21. C
22. A
23. B
24. C
25. B

# TEST 2

DIRECTIONS: Each question or incomplete statement is followed by several suggested answers or completions. Select the one that BEST answers the question or completes the statement. *PRINT THE LETTER OF THE CORRECT ANSWER IN THE SPACE AT THE RIGHT.*

1. Software responsible for executing other software is called a(n)  1.____
   A. application software
   B. operating system
   C. utility software
   D. toolkit

2. A compiler is a type of _____ software.  2.____
   A. translation     B. application     C. operating     D. mixing

3. The _____ provides all the capabilities to develop software.  3.____
   A. notepad
   B. wordpad
   C. adobe reader
   D. IDE

4. Missing parenthesis and delimiters lead to a _____ error.  4.____
   A. syntax     B. logical     C. sensible     D. runtime

5. The _____ error is the most difficult to identify.  5.____
   A. syntax     B. logical     C. compile time     D. runtime

6. 
   ```
   private void checkFor(){
       int a = 1;
       for(;a<10;){
           System.out.println(a);
       }
   }
   ```
   What will be the output of the above code?  6.____
   A. Error in for loop syntax
   B. Runtime error as increment statement is missing
   C. Code prints 1 to 9 digits
   D. Code prints 1 infinite times

7. If a method has a return type 'void,' it means method returns  7.____
   A. nothing
   B. null
   C. an empty object
   D. 0

8. Which of the following is invalid for a loop statement?  8.____
   A. int a=0; for(;a<10-; a++){}
   B. for(int a = 1, b = 2; a < 10; a++){}
   C. for(int a = 1, b = 9; a < 10; a++,b++){}
   D. for(;false;){}

9. The _____ statement is used to stop the current iteration of the loop.  9.____
   A. continue     B. break     C. return     D. stop

10. Java uses the _____ value of character during comparison.
    A. UTF8    B. UNICODE    C. ASCII    D. UTF-16

11. Primitive return types do not accept _____ value.
    A. signed    B. negative    C. character    D. null

12. A method whose return type is object reference can return sub type object reference, the returning type is called _____ return.
    A. null    B. primitive    C. covariant    D. shallow

13. Which of the following statements is CORRECT?
    A. It is legal to add an empty return statement in a method whose return type is void
    B. The method having returned type object reference cannot return null
    C. The array is a perfect legal type to declare in method signature only
    D. Overloaded method does not change return type

14. private List check(){
        ArrayList list = new ArrayList();
        list = null          //Line 1
        return list;         //Line 2
    }
    What will be the output of the above code?
    A. The null object of subtype cannot be returned
    B. Compile time error on Line 2; subtype cannot be returned
    C. Program crashes at runtime at Line 1
    D. The method is successfully compiled and executed

15. public class TestReturn {
        public static void main(String{} args){
            TestReturn.emptyReturn(2);
        }
        private static void emptyReturn(int a){
            a + = 10;                    //Line 1
            return;                      //Line 2
            System.out.println(a);       //Line 3
        }
    What will be the output of the above code?
    A. The program is successfully compiled and executed and prints 12
    B. It is illegal to use a return statement in a method whose return type is void
    C. No return value is given at Line 2
    D. Syntax error at Line 3, unreachable code

16. Suppose an int array declare as int[] ar = {}; what will be the result when the following line is executed: System.out.println(ar[0]);?
    A. Program throws NullPointerException
    B. Compile time error
    C. Array's hex code prints
    D. The statement throws ArrayIndexOutOfBoundsException

17. String[] str = new String [4];
    What will be the output by the above statement?
    A. Four String objects created
    B. One String array created with 4 String objects
    C. Only one String array created
    D. It is illegal to create String array

18. ```
    public class ArrayTest{
        public static void main(String[] args)}
            int[] nums = new int[10];
            for(int a = 0, b = 0; a < 20; a++){
                if(a%2 = = 0){
                nums[b] = a;
                ++b;
                }
            }
            for(int a = 0; a < nums.length-1; a++){
                System.out.print(nums[a] + " ");
            }
        }
    }
    ```
    What will be the output of the above code?
    A. 0 2 4 6 8 10 12 14 16
    B. 0 2 3 4 8 13
    C. 1 3 5 7 9
    D. 1 1 2 3 5 6

19. ```
    public class OverloadTest {
        public static void main(String[] args){
            System.out.println("main 1");
        }
        public static void main(String[] args){
            System.out.println("main 2");
        }
    }
    ```
    What will be the output of the above code?
    A. main 1 main 2
    B. main 1
    C. Compile time error, main method cannot be overloaded
    D. Runtime error

20. Which of the following statements is NOT true for String object?
    A. String object is immutable
    B. String object reference is immutable
    C. String class cannot be extended
    D. String literals store in the pool

21. Class members with _____ modifier are accessible in their own package as well as in derived classes.
    A. default    B. public    C. protected    D. private

22. How does a field make read-only?
    A. By prefixing the field with the read-only keyword
    B. Make mutator method private
    C. Set variable as final
    D. Mark field as static

    22.____

23. A(n) _____ keyword is used to keep the method from overriding.
    A. abstract    B. final    C. static    D. private

    23.____

24. The characteristic of an OOP in which object can refer to one of its derived class is called
    A. generalization          B. aggregation
    C. collection              D. polymorphism

    24.____

25. If a class holds an instance of another class, this relation falls in the _____ concept.
    A. IS-A        B. HAS-A        C. HAVE-A        D. ARE-A

    25.____

---

## KEY (CORRECT ANSWERS)

1. B
2. A
3. D
4. A
5. B

6. D
7. A
8. D
9. A
10. B

11. D
12. C
13. A
14. D
15. D

16. D
17. C
18. A
19. C
20. B

21. C
22. B
23. B
24. D
25. B

# TEST 3

DIRECTIONS: Each question or incomplete statement is followed by several suggested answers or completions. Select the one that BEST answers the question or completes the statement. *PRINT THE LETTER OF THE CORRECT ANSWER IN THE SPACE AT THE RIGHT.*

1. The compiler is unable to identify a _____ error.
   A. syntax
   B. logical
   C. compile time
   D. runtime

   1.____

2. Long literals postfix with
   A. L
   B. Long
   C. i
   D. Li

   2.____

3. The _____ datatype supports binary, octal and hexadecimal literals.
   A. short
   B. float
   C. integer
   D. boolean

   3.____

4. Which one of the statements is CORRECT when initializing boolean?
   boolean b =
   A. 'false'
   B. 0
   C. /1
   D. true

   4.____

5. What is the CORRECT way to initialize float?
   float f =
   A. 4.0
   B. 4
   C. 4d
   D. 4.0

   5.____

6. 'operator' _____ the operands if one of the operands is a strong.
   A. add
   B. subtract
   C. convert String into int
   D. concat

   6.____

7. ```
   private void checkString(){
       String str = "11";      //Line 1
       int num = str + 2       //Line 2
   }
   ```
   What will be the output of the above code?
   A. A type mismatch error occurs on Line 2 at compile time
   B. A type mismatch error occurs on Line 2 at runtime
   C. Variable str auto casts at runtime and added to 2 and set 14 in num
   D. Variable str auto casts at runtime and added to 2 and set 112 in num

   7.____

8. The _____ operator returns the opposite boolean value of an evaluated expression.
   A. ternary
   B. inversion
   C. rational
   D. increment

   8.____

9. The occurrence of abnormal condition that alters normal program behavior is called
   A. exception
   B. error
   C. bug
   D. defect

   9.____
   ```

10. A block of code responsible for handling exception is called  10.____
    A. throw block                    B. error handler
    C. exception handler              D. catch handler

11. The _____ variable is lived until its method is on the stack.  11.____
    A. local        B. instance      C. static       D. temporary

12. ```
    public class InstanceScope {
        int inst = 1;
        public static void main(String[] args) {
            inst++;                         //Line 1
            {
                int inst = 10;              //Line 2
            }
            System.out.println(inst);       //Line 2
        }
    }
    ```
    What will be the output of the above code?
    The program will
    A. compile but at runtime crash on Line 1
    B. not compile due to an error on Line 1 and Line 2
    C. not compile due to an error on Line 1 only
    D. successfully compile and run
    
    12.____

13. _____ variable is alive until block execution completes.  13.____
    A. Block        B. Temporary     C. Class        D. Instance

14. Which of the following statements BEST define overloading?  14.____
    A. Overloading is defined as a method having the same name, same parameter type, but the number of parameters is different
    B. Overloading is a re-use of an already defined method name, but different parameter types
    C. The method is called overloaded if its return type must be the same with the already defined method
    D. If a method has the same signature with the already defined method, it is called overloading

15. Suppose there is a method overloadMe and it is defined as:  15.____
        void overloadMe(float f, String s) throws MalformedInput Exception {}
    Which one of the following declarations does NOT comply with overloading rules and gets an error?
    A. void overloadMe(String s, float f) throws NumberFormatException {}
    B. void overloadMe(float f, String s) throws NumberFormatException {}
    C. int overloadMe(double f, String s) throws IOException {return 0;}
    D. void overloadMe(char ch) throws ArrayIndexOutOfBoundsException {}
    ```

16.  ```
     public class StringTest {
         public static void main(String{} args) {
             String str = "s";
             if(str.startsWith("s"))
                 str + = "art";
             if(str = = "starts")
                 str + = "true";
             System.out.println(str);
         }
     }
     ```
     What will be the output of the above code?
     A. start    B. true    C. starttrue    C. strue

17.  ```
     public class StringTest {
         public static void main(String[] args) }
             String[] sArray = {"day", "weekday", "month");
             for(int i  = 1; i < sArray.length-1; i++) {
                 System.out.println(sArray[i].toUpperCase());
             }
         }
     }
     ```
     What will be the output of the above code?
     A. WEEKDAYMONTH           B. DAYWEEKDAY
     C. WEEKDAY                D. MONTH

18.  Which of the methods is used to get the single character from string on giving index?
     A. substring()    B. charAt()    C. chatAT()    D. get()

19.  ```
     public class StringTest {
         public static void main(String[] args) {
             String str = "Map";
             int i = 1;
             System.out.println(str + = i);
         }
     }
     ```
     What will be the output of the above code?
     A. Compile time error         B. Runtime error
     C. Map1                       D. 1Map1

20.  ```
     public class StringTest {
         public static void main(String[] args) {
             String s1 = "abc", s2 = "abc";
             String s3 = new String("abc");
             String s4 = new String("abc");
             System.out.print(s1 = = s2);
             System.out.print(s3 = = s4);
         }
     }
     ```

What will be the output of the above code?
A. true false   B. false false   C. true true   D. false true

21. In inheritance, members with _____ modifiers cannot be inherited.                    21._____
    A. public   B. protected   C. default   D. private

22. A method that is used to initialize object state is called a                          22._____
    A. method   B. field   C. constructor   D. destructor

23. public class A {                                                                      23._____
        public A(){
        system.out.print("inside A");
        }
    }
    public class B extends A {
        public B(){
        System.out.println("inside B");
        }
    }
    public class TestConstructorCalling {
        public static void main(String[] args) {
        A b = new B();
        }
    }
    What will be the output of the above code?
    A. inside A inside B          B. inside B inside A
    C. inside A                   D. inside B

24. With reference to the above class TestConstructorCalling, class B called its          24._____
    super class A constructor when its object is initialized. This process is called
    A. calling parent constructor      B. constructor queue
    C. constructor chaining            D. invoking parent

25. A(n) _____ class has a constructor, but it cannot be instantiated.                    25._____
    A. abstract   B. concrete   C. enum   D. aspect

## KEY (CORRECT ANSWERS)

1. B
2. A
3. C
4. D
5. B

6. D
7. A
8. B
9. A
10. C

11. A
12. B
13. A
14. B
15. B

16. A
17. C
18. B
19. C
20. A

21. D
22. C
23. A
24. C
25. A

# TEST 4

DIRECTIONS: Each question or incomplete statement is followed by several suggested answers or completions. Select the one that BEST answers the question or completes the statement. *PRINT THE LETTER OF THE CORRECT ANSWER IN THE SPACE AT THE RIGHT.*

1. The effect of reusing a variable that is already declared is called  1.____
   A. reusability   B. accessing   C. shadowing   D. reinitializing

2. ```
   void check(){
       int a = 10;          //Line 1
       float f = 0f;        //Line 2
       short s = 327687     //Line 3
       char c = 'a';        //Line 4
   }
   ```
   In checking out the above function, which line shows a syntax error?  2.____
   A. 1   B. 2   C. 3   D. 4

3. When creating an object using the syntax (Object obj = new Object();), what does JVM do?  3.____
   A. Declare a reference variable obj
   B. Create an object on the stack
   C. Declare and assign reference
   D. Make a reference, create a new object, and assign a reference to obj

4. Which of the following is the correct way to assign octal value to int?  4.____
   int i =
   A. 01   B. 0X1   C. OCT1   D. 1O

5. What will happen when the following statement executes?  5.____
   Object obj = null;
   A. Creates an object that holds a null constant
   B. Creates space for obj reference variable
   C. Initializes object with null value
   D. Initializes object with general type
   ```

6.    private static void checkDoWhile(){
        int a = 2, b = 1;
        String s = " ";

        do{
           switch(a){
           case 3:
              s + = a;
              break;
           case 5:
              s.concat("Hello");
           case 7:
              s + = " "+ a;
           }
           ++a;
           b++;
        }while(b<10);
        System.out.println(s);
      }
What will be the result of variable 's' when following the executed code?
A.  3 5 7          B.  5 8 Hello     C.  Hello 1 2 3     D.  1 3 5 Hello 9

7.    private void checkTryCatch(String b){
        try {
           b + = "try block";
           char c = b.charAt(5);
        } catch (IndexOutOfBoundsException e) {
           b.concat("-exception caught. " + e.getMessage());
           return;
        }finally{
           b.concat("-Ah finally in finally block");
        }
        System.out.println(b);
      }
What will be the output when the above method executes with argument "Inside"?
A. Inside try block
B. Inside try block – exception caught.IndexOutOfBoundsException
C. Try block – Ah finally in finally block
D. Try block – exception – Ah finally in finally block

8.    Which of the following is the CORRECT while loop expression?
      A. int a = 0; while(a){}          B. while("true"){}
      C. while(1){}                     D. while(false){}

9. 
```
public static void ternaryTest(){
    float a = 14.0f;
    String s = (a < 10)? "happy":a > 15)?"world":"today";
    System.out.println(s);
}
```
What will be the output of the above code?
   A. happy
   B. world
   C. today
   D. It is illegal to compare a float with an int

10. The _____ clause is used to tell the JVM what action takes when exception throws.
   A. try   B. finally   C. threw   D. catch

11. The only condition when the finally block does not invoke is when
   A. the JVM executes system.exit() statement
   B. return statement executes in try block
   C. break statement executes in try block
   D. catch block throws an exception

12. The compiler enforces _____ exception to be handled.
   A. runtime   B. checked   C. unchecked   D. compiler

13. _____ is the superclass of all exceptions and returns.
   A. Throwable           B. Error
   C. JVM Exception       D. Defecto

14. What exception will throw when the following line of code is executed?
   Float f = new Float("abc");
   A. IllegalInputStatement      B. NumberCastException
   C. NumberFormatException      D. ClassCastException

15. To call a superclass overridden method, _____ keyword is used.
   A. this   B. super   C. abstract   D. final

16. 
```
public interface TestInterface {
    public abstract void implementMe(int i);
}
```
What will be the CORRECT class definition when it implements the above interface?
   A. abstract class IClass implements TestInterface{}
   B. class IClass extends TestInterface{
          public void implementMe(){}
      }

C. class IClass implements TestInterface {
    public void implementMe(String s) {}
}
D. class IClass implements TestInterface {
    public abstract void implementMe(int i);
}

17. Every object of class has its own copy of _____ method.  17._____
    A. static    B. local    C. instance    D. final

18.
```java
public class B {
    static int a;
    int x;
    static void show(){
        x = 9;          //Line 1
    }
    void print(){
        a = 10;         //Line 2
    }
}
```
18._____

What will happen when the above program is compiled?
A. Compile time error at Line 1
B. Compile time error at Line 2
C. Compile time error at both Line 1 and Line 2
D. No compile time error

19.
```java
public class Animal{
    public void getSound(){
    System.out.print("animal sound-");
    }
}
class Dog extends Animal{
    public void getSound(){
    super.getSound();
    System.out.print("barked");
    }
}
class Cat extends Animal{
    public void getSound(){
    super.getSound();
    System.out.print("meow");
    }
}
```
19._____

```
class TestAnimal{
    public static void main(String[] args)}
    Animal an = new dog();
    an.getSound();
    an – new Cat();
    an.getSound();
    }
}
```
What will be the output of the above code?
A. barked meow
B. barked barked
C. animal sound – barked animal sound – meow
D. barked animal sound - meow

20. A _____ object represents existing file or directory.  20._____
    A. File  B. Directory  C. FileInstance  D. SystemFile

21. The IO related files are found in _____ package.  21._____
    A. Java.net  B. Java.io
    C. Java.inputoutput  D. Javax.io

22. Which one of the following is NOT a member of Java.io package?  22._____
    A. Writer  B. Reader
    C. ObjectInput  D. DirectoryFilter

23.
```
public class OverloadTest{
    public static void main(String[] args){
        overloadMe(40.4f);              //Line 1
        overloadMe(40);                 //Line 2
        overloadMe("Method Overloaded"); //Line 3
    }
    static void overloadMe(String s){
        System.out.println(s);
    }
    static void overloadMe(float f){
        System.out.println(f);
    }
}
```
23._____

What will be the output of the above code?
A. Syntax error at Line 2, no overloaded method defines for an int type parameter
B. 40.4
   40
   Method Overloaded
C. 40.4
   Method Overloaded
D. 40.4
   40.0
   Method Overloaded

24. 
```
public class OverloadTest{
    public static void main(String[] args){
        overloadMe(40.4);
    }
    static void overloadMe(int i){
        System.out.print(i);
    }
    static void overloadMe(float f){
        System.out.print(f);
    }
}
```
What will be the output of the above code?
A. Compile time error  
B. Runtime error  
C. 40  
D. 40 40.4

25. 
```
public class OverloadTest{
    public static void main(String[] args){
        int a = overloadMe(40);
    }
    static int overloadMe(int i){
        System.out.println(i);
        return i;
    }
    static float overloadMe(int i){
        System.out.println(i);
        return i;
    }
}
```
What will be the output of the above code?
A. 40 40  
B. 40  
C. Compile time error  
D. Runtime error

## KEY (CORRECT ANSWERS)

1. C
2. C
3. D
4. A
5. B

6. A
7. A
8. D
9. C
10. D

11. A
12. B
13. A
14. C
15. B

16. A
17. C
18. A
19. C
20. A

21. B
22. D
23. D
24. A
25. C

# EXAMINATION SECTION
# TEST 1

DIRECTIONS: Each question or incomplete statement is followed by several suggested answers or completions. Select the one the BEST answers the question or completes the statement. *PRINT THE LETTER OF THE CORRECT ANSWER IN THE SPACE AT THE RIGHT.*

1. Which of the following was an advantage associated with open source software in the 1990s?

    A. A standard user interface for productivity applications such as word processing and spreadsheets
    B. Stringent quality control processes
    C. Suitability for mission-critical applications
    D. A broadened community of programmers who can stabilize and add functionality to software

    1.____

2. IP addresses

    I. are attached to every node on the Internet
    II. are sometimes listed as a character string
    III. establish a direct link between sender and recipient
    IV. use circuit-switching technology

    A. I only
    B. I and II
    C. II, III and IV
    D. I, II, III and IV

    2.____

3. Programming languages used exclusively for artificial intelligence applications include

    A. AIML and Prolog
    B. LISP and Prolog
    C. Ada and LISP
    D. Delphi and Python

    3.____

4. Cookies are usually stored by browsers as

    A. text files
    B. algorithms
    C. tokens
    D. HTML files

    4.____

5. Analysts typically use each of the following to evaluate the flow of data through an information system, EXCEPT

    A. decision trees
    B. Gantt charts
    C. structured English
    D. data flow diagrams

    5.____

6. Methods for protecting a computer system from viruses include
    I. accessing a Web site that offers on-line virus scans

    6.____

43

II. checking physical media, such as floppy disks or DVDs, before they are used in a computer
III. erecting a firewall
IV. never opening e-mail attachments from people unknown to the user

A. I and IV
B. II, III and IV
C. III and IV only
D. I, II, III and IV

7. Describing an algorithm as "general" means that it

A. does not have a clear stopping point
B. addresses the stated problem in all instances
C. can be carried out in any sequence
D. can be expressed in any language

8. Packet-switching offers each of the following advantages, EXCEPT

A. faster transmission of data
B. greater network user capacity
C. greater degree of redundancy
D. more localized data corruption

9. The term "digital divide" describes the discrepancies between

A. people who have access to, and the resources to use, new information and communication technologies, and people who do not
B. approximations in the values of floating-point numbers by a processor
C. the rate at which computer processing speeds increase and the rate at which the capacity to store data increases
D. data that is entered into a database application and the information that is displayed to an end-user

10. The main advantage of using programmable microcode is that

A. programs can be made very small and portable
B. the CPU's capacity is never overclocked
C. the same instructions can be executed on different hardware platforms
D. it is usually executed more quickly than other program code

11. Cache memory is NOT

A. used only in large computers
B. used to solve the problem of inadequate primary memory
C. divided into the two main categories of RAM cache and secondary cache
D. used to improve processing speed

12. When PC users ask for a document to be sent to them, they should request a .txt file, because it

A. comes with a built-in antivirus program
B. will only transmit text

C. denotes a disinfected file
D. cannot contain malicious and executable code

13. Line personnel in an organization can enter transaction data and see totals and other results immediately by use of _____ processing     13.____

    A. summary
    B. batch
    C. on-line
    D. real-time

14. A network with a main computer that does all of the processing for a number of simple display units is described as     14.____

    A. peer-to-peer
    B. client-file server
    C. n-tier
    D. terminal emulation

15. All buses consist of two parts, the _____ bus and the _____ bus.     15.____

    A. internal; external
    B. main; expansion
    C. ISA; PCI
    D. address; data

16. The _____ is a small amount of high-speed memory that stores regularly used data.     16.____

    A. cache
    B. spool
    C. buffer
    D. frame

17. Technological cornerstones of the Internet include each of the following, EXCEPT     17.____

    A. HTML
    B. TCP/IP
    C. URL
    D. MMDS

18. The OSI (Open System Interconnection) model defines a networking framework for implementing protocols in seven layers. The _____ layer, or layer 3, provides switching and routing technologies, creating logical paths, known as virtual circuits, for transmitting data from node to node     18.____

    A. network
    B. presentation
    C. transport
    D. session

19. The main difference between the Windows NT operating system and the current Windows OS is that the NT operating system

    A. has no relationship to MS-DOS
    B. has a different user interface
    C. runs faster
    D. supports more peripheral devices

19.____

20. Before sound can be handled on a computer, it must first be converted to electrical energy, and then transformed through an analog-to-digital converter into a digital representation. _____ Law states that the more often a sound wave is sampled, the more accurate the digital representation.

    A. Gilder's
    B. Moore's
    C. Amdahl's
    D. Nyquist's

20.____

21. The primary disadvantage associated with interpreted programming languages, such as Java, is that they

    A. present fewer solutions to individual problems
    B. have slower execution speeds
    C. are not as portable
    D. are more difficult for programmers to understand

21.____

22. The advantages promised by the emerging technology of holographic storage include
    I. higher storage densities
    II. easier synchronization with the CPU
    III. non-volatility
    IV. faster data transfer speeds

    A. I only
    B. I and IV
    C. II and III
    D. III and IV

22.____

23. A file that contains instructions in a particular computer's machine language is said to contain _____ code.

    A. macro
    B. object
    C. scripting
    D. source

23.____

24. A computer uses _____ to transform raw data into useful information.

    A. input devices and output devices
    B. a processor and memory
    C. memory and a motherboard
    D. language and protocols

24.____

25. In computer graphics, the term "raster graphics" is synonymous with    25.____

    A. vector graphics
    B. bitmapped graphics
    C. object-oriented graphics
    D. autosizing

26. In 1996, journalist and former White House Press Secretary Pierre Salinger, making a    26.____
    public statement about the causes of the recent TWA Flight 800 crash, became the figurehead for what is now known as the "Pierre Salinger Syndrome" This phenomenon refers to the

    A. act of hiding information by embedding messages within another
    B. pit those who have the skills, knowledge and abilities to use the technologies against those who do not
    C. tendency to believe that everything one reads on the Internet is true
    D. practice of using software to monitor the behavior of a user visiting a Web site or sending an e-mail

27. Which of the following is NOT a term that is interchangeable with "expansion card"?    27.____

    A. Expansion file
    B. Expansion board
    C. Adapter
    D. Socket

28. Multidimensional database management systems are also referred to as    28.____

    A. Relational database management systems
    B. On-line Transaction Processing (OLTP)
    C. SQL servers
    D. On-line Analytical Processing (OLAP)

29. The primary difference between "smart" and "dumb" printers is that    29.____

    A. smart printers can perform dithering
    B. smart printers use a page description language
    C. dumb printers use less system memory
    D. dumb printers cannot bitmap vector graphics

30. The interface between the CPU and the hard disk's electronics is known as the hard disk    30.____

    A. navigator
    B. manager
    C. reticulate
    D. controller

31. A single _____ port can be used to connect as many as 127 peripheral devices to a    31.____
    computer.

    A. PIA
    B. Fire Wire
    C. parallel
    D. USB

32. In the binary system, 1011 equals a decimal  32.___

    A. 2
    B. 3
    C. 11
    D. 12

33. A transistor radio is an example of _____ transmission of data  33.___

    A. half-duplex
    B. full-duplex
    C. half-simplex
    D. simplex

34. Which of the following is NOT a type of liquid crystal display?  34.___

    A. Active matrix
    B. Passive matrix
    C. Electroluminescent
    D. Dual-scan

35. Which of the following is a term for commercial software that has been pirated and made available to the public via a bulletin board system (BBS) or the Internet?  35.___

    A. Freeware
    B. Crackware
    C. Warez
    D. Shareware

36. IBM-compatible PCs denote the primary hard disk with the  36.___

    A. number 1
    B. letter A
    C. letter C
    D. letter X

37. Each of the following operating systems provides some kind of graphical user interface, EXCEPT  37.___

    A. Macintosh OS
    B. Linux
    C. UNIX
    D. DOS

38. An operating system's overall quality is most often judged on its ability to manage  38.___

    A. program execution
    B. device drivers
    C. disk utilities
    D. application backup

39. In multimedia product development, elements of a program are arranged into separate  39.___

    A. tracks
    B. columns

C. zones
D. layers

40. The CPU contains the _____ unit.
    I. I/O
    II. control
    III. arithmetic
    IV. instructing decoding

    A. I and II
    B. I, II and IV
    C. II and V
    D. I, II, III and IV

41. The on-line application that locates and displays the document associated with a hyper-link is a(n)

    A. server
    B. plug-in
    C. browser
    D. finder

42. Which of the following devices requires a driver?
    I. printer
    II. mouse
    III. DVD drive
    IV. keyboard

    A. I only
    B. I, II and IV
    C. II and IV
    D. I, II, III and IV

43. Database management systems include each of the following components, EXCEPT

    A. data collection applications
    B. statistical analysis applications
    C. data modification applications
    D. query languages

44. Waves are characterized by each of the following, EXCEPT

    A. Frequency
    B. Pulse
    C. Frequency
    D. Amplitude

45. Although considered to be outdated by many programmers, _____ is still the most widely used programming language in the world.

    A. Pascal
    B. COBOL
    C. FORTRAN
    D. BASIC

46. A graphics program using the _____ model represents three-dimensional objects by displaying their outlines and edges.  46.___

    A. wireframe
    B. volumetric
    C. solid
    D. surface

47. The concept central to the legislation that regulates telephone service in the United States is  47.___

    A. broadband service
    B. consumer price parity
    C. reasonable access time
    D. universal access

48. In order to be certified as "open source" by the Open Source Institute (OSI), a program must meet each of the following criteria, EXCEPT that the  48.___

    A. rights attached to the program are contingent on the program's being part of a particular software distribution
    B. author or holder of the license of the source code cannot collect royalties on the distribution of the program
    C. distributed program must make the source code accessible to the user
    D. licensed software cannot place restrictions on other software distributed with it

49. Ethernet systems typically use a _____ topology.  49.___

    A. bus
    B. star
    C. ring
    D. tree

50. In enterprises, the _____ is the computer that routes the traffic from a workstation to the outside network that is serving the Web pages.  50.___

    A. proxy server
    B. ISP
    C. packet switcher
    D. gateway

## KEY (CORRECT ANSWERS)

| | | | | |
|---|---|---|---|---|
| 1. D | 11. A | 21. B | 31. D | 41. C |
| 2. B | 12. D | 22. B | 32. C | 42. D |
| 3. B | 13. C | 23. B | 33. D | 43. A |
| 4. A | 14. A | 24. B | 34. C | 44. B |
| 5. B | 15. D | 25. B | 35. C | 45. B |
| 6. D | 16. A | 26. C | 36. C | 46. A |
| 7. B | 17. D | 27. D | 37. D | 47. D |
| 8. A | 18. A | 28. D | 38. A | 48. A |
| 9. A | 19. A | 29. B | 39. A | 49. A |
| 10. C | 20. D | 30. D | 40. B | 50. D |

# TEST 2

DIRECTIONS: Each question or incomplete statement is followed by several suggested answers or completions. Select the one the BEST answers the question or completes the statement. *PRINT THE LETTER OF THE CORRECT ANSWER IN THE SPACE AT THE RIGHT.*

1. "Refresh rate" typically refers to the

    A. number of times RAM is updated in a second
    B. time it takes to completely rewrite a disk
    C. number of times the display monitor is redrawn in a second
    D. time it takes for a Web pages to reload

    1.____

2. In a markup language, authors use _____ to identify portions of a document.

    A. icons
    B. schemas
    C. numbers
    D. elements

    2.____

3. Object-oriented programming languages rely heavily on _____ to create high-level objects.
    
    I. formalization
    II. abstraction
    III. information hiding
    IV. encapsulation

    A. I only
    B. I, II and III
    C. II, III and IV
    D. I, II, III and IV

    3.____

4. The base unit of three-dimensional graphics is the

    A. texel
    B. voxel
    C. pixel
    D. bit

    4.____

5. In computing, "gamma correction" typically refers to an adjustment in the

    A. light intensity of a scanner, monitor, or printer
    B. amplitude modulation
    C. emission of gamma waves by a CRT monitor
    D. speed with which analog data is digitized

    5.____

6. The OSI (Open System Interconnection) model defines a networking framework for implementing protocols in seven layers. The seventh layer of the OSI model consists of the

    A. hardware
    B. applications

    6.____

C. protocols
D. network

7. A significant difference between frame switching packet switching is that frame switching

    A. offers accelerated packet processing
    B. creates a virtual circuit
    C. allows multiple connections on the same set of hardware
    D. contains now quality-of-service assurances

7.____

8. In _____ memory, each location has an actual "address."

    A. RAM
    B. ROM
    C. PROM
    D. EPROM

8.____

9. Video applications require a bare minimum of _____ frames per second in order to function.

    A. 8
    B. 15
    C. 30
    D. 60

9.____

10. The most commonly used network application today is

    A. Web design
    B. BBS
    C. e-mail
    D. software downloading

10.____

11. Standardized codes for representing character data numerically include
    I. ANSI
    II. EBCDIC
    III. ASCII
    IV. DECS

    A. I and II
    B. II and III
    C. II, III and IV
    D. I, II, III and IV

11.____

12. Photolithography is the process of transferring geometric shapes on a mask to the surface of a silicon wafer. Possible future alternative technologies to photolithography include each of the following, EXCEPT the

    A. multiple-wave laser beam
    B. electron beam
    C. extreme ultraviolet
    D. X-ray

12.____

13. Hard disk mechanisms typically contain a single

    A. head actuator
    B. read/write head
    C. platter
    D. landing zone

14. Contemporary Rapid Application Development (RAD) emphasizes the reduction of development time through

    A. trimming code
    B. inserting pre-written artificial intelligence capabilities
    C. establishing a graphical user interface
    D. making slight modifications to proprietary software

15. A Web site contains a number of databases that contain all the information about an organization's clients-such as names, addresses, credit card information, past invoices, etc.). This is an example of a data

    A. mine
    B. warehouse
    C. dictionary
    D. mart

16. Currently, a computer's most difficult task would be to

    A. speak in long paragraphs
    B. recognize spoken words
    C. interpret the meaning of words
    D. compose a syntactically correct item of discourse

17. An API is a(n)

    A. algorithm for the lossless compression of files
    B. set of routines, protocols, and tools for building software applications
    C. piece of software that helps the operating system communicate with a peripheral device
    D. code for representing characters as numbers

18. The disadvantages associated with ring LAN topologies include
    I. more limited geographical range
    II. low bandwidth
    III. high expense
    IV. complex and difficult installation

    A. I only
    B. I and II
    C. III and IV
    D. I, II, III and IV

19. Scientists would most likely use _____ to analyze variations in planetary orbits.

    A. a mainframe
    B. the Internet

C. a supercomputer
D. a virtual network

20. The primary disadvantage to shared-memory multiprocessing involves

    A. slow retrieval speeds
    B. bus overload
    C. inadequate trace width
    D. RAM purges

21. If a computer user enters a legal command that does not make any sense in the given context, the user has committed an error of

    A. syntax
    B. semantics
    C. formatting
    D. parsing

22. Which of the following terms is NOT synonymous with the others?

    A. Floating point unit
    B. Numeric coprocessor
    C. Math coprocessor
    D. Accelerator board

23. Which of the following is a measure of data transfer capacity?

    A. Duplication rate
    B. Bandwidth
    C. Frequency
    D. Baud rate

24. In the 1990s, the main obstacle to the use of the Linux operating system in desktop applications was

    A. the lack of a standard user interface
    B. difficulties in file and print serving
    C. inability to accommodate multiple platforms
    D. insufficient support from the commercial sector

25. Which of the following external bus standards supports "hot plugging"–the ability to add and remove devices to a computer while the computer is running and have the operating system automatically recognize the change?

    A. Serial
    B. USB
    C. PCI
    D. Parallel port

26. When a key on a computer keyboard is struck, each of the following may occur, EXCEPT

    A. a cursor on the screen moves
    B. a scan code is sent to an application

C. a binary number is input into the computer
D. an EBCDIC code for a letter is sent to a word processing application

27. SONET

    A. cannot be used to link digital networks to fiber optics
    B. is a synchronous Layer 1 protocol
    C. prohibits data streams of different speeds from being multiplexed in the same line
    D. can scale up to 4 Gbps

28. A user handles data stored on a disk with the utility program known as the

    A. file sorter
    B. file manager
    C. disk scanner
    D. finder

29. A _____ is a tool that helps users of word processing or desktop publishing applications to avoid formatting complex documents individually.

    A. merge
    B. column
    C. template
    D. table

30. Which of the following is a high-level programming language that is particularly suited for use on the World Wide Web, often through the use of small, downloadable applications known as applets?

    A. XML
    B. Ada
    C. Java
    D. C++

31. Microprocessor speeds have increased dramatically over the past two decades, largely as a result of significant

    A. improvements in hardware breakpoints
    B. increases in trace depth
    C. compression of overlay RAM
    D. reductions in trace width

32. On most PCs, this contains all the code required to control the keyboard, display screen, disk drives, serial communications, and a number of miscellaneous functions.

    A. Flash memory
    B. Operating system
    C. BIOS
    D. USB

33. Which of the following is a rating system originally designed to help parents and teachers control what children access on the Internet, but now also used to facilitate other uses for labels, including code signing and privacy?

    A. V-chip
    B. Recreational Software Advisory Council
    C. Platform for Internet Content Selection
    D. Cyber Patrol

34. A database designed for continuous addition and deletion of records is said to perform the function of _____ processing.

    A. batch
    B. drilldown
    C. transaction
    D. analytical

35. A unique 128-bit number, produced by the Windows OS or by some Windows applications to identify a particular component, application, file, database entry, and/or user is known as a

    A. key
    B. GUID
    C. PGP
    D. DLL

36. Compared to private-key cryptograph, public-key

    A. uses two keys
    B. is easier to understand
    C. functions more smoothly with contemporary networks
    D. requires fewer computations

37. Static RAM (SRAM) is used to

    A. supplement the main memory
    B. determine which information should be kept in the cache
    C. form the memory cache
    D. form the disk cache

38. A(n) _____ system is used to produce reports that will help managers throughout an organization to evaluate their departments.

    A. expert
    B. management information
    C. office automation
    D. transaction processing

39. Software that may be delivered/downloaded and used without charge, but is nevertheless still copyrighted by the author, is known as

    A. public-domain software
    B. shareware

C. open-source software
D. freeware

40. Barriers to widespread use of cable modems in Internet access include
   I. the one-way transmission design of the television infrastructure
   II. uncertain capacity of television infrastructure
   III. complexity of protocols
   IV. bandwidth restrictions

   A. I only
   B. I and II
   C. II and IV
   D. I, II, III and IV

41. Which of the following is NOT a function that can be performed with a spreadsheet application?

   A. Budget charts and graphs
   B. Inventory management
   C. Audiovisual presentations
   D. Fiscal forecasting

42. Which of the following is a Windows-based graphical user interface for the UNIX operating system?

   A. Linux
   B. Gnu
   C. MOTIF
   D. UNI

43. In a database, the _____ contains a code, number, name, or some other information that uniquely identifies the record.

   A. primary key
   B. file
   C. schema
   D. key field

44. Which of the following terms is NOT synonymous with the others?

   A. Web bug
   B. Clear GIF
   C. Web beacon
   D. Cookie

45. As a firewall technology, the proxy server operates by

   A. examining each packet that enters or exits a network, and accepts or rejects it based on a given set of rules
   B. applying security mechanisms to specific applications
   C. constantly changing its location
   D. intercepting all messages entering and leaving a network

46. VRAM is a specific kind of memory used to

    A. accelerate processing speeds
    B. store video display data
    C. create virtual addresses, rather than real addresses, to store data and instructions
    D. create a virtual environment for the user

47. Which phase of the application development process serves to identify features that must be added to the program to make it satisfactory to users?

    A. Software concept
    B. Coding and debugging
    C. System testing
    D. Requirements analysis

48. What is the term for the natural data size of a computer?

    A. Word size
    B. Clock speed
    C. Bus width
    D. Cache

49. Microkernels operate by moving many of the operating system services into "user space" that other operating systems keep in the kernel. This migration tends to have each of the following effects, EXCEPT greater

    A. security
    B. bug immunity for the kernel
    C. configurability
    D. "fixed" memory footprint

50. High-level programming languages are
    I. useful when speed is essential
    II. processor-independent
    III. usually compiled or assembled
    IV. easier to read, write and maintain than other languages

    A. I and IV
    B. I, II, and III
    C. II, III and IV
    D. I, II, III and IV

## KEY (CORRECT ANSWERS)

| | | | | |
|---|---|---|---|---|
| 1. C | 11. C | 21. B | 31. D | 41. C |
| 2. D | 12. A | 22. D | 32. C | 42. C |
| 3. C | 13. A | 23. B | 33. C | 43. A |
| 4. A | 14. C | 24. A | 34. C | 44. D |
| 5. A | 15. B | 25. B | 35. B | 45. D |
| 6. B | 16. C | 26. D | 36. A | 46. B |
| 7. B | 17. B | 27. B | 37. C | 47. C |
| 8. A | 18. C | 28. B | 38. B | 48. A |
| 9. B | 19. C | 29. C | 39. C | 49. D |
| 10. C | 20. B | 30. C | 40. B | 50. C |

# EXAMINATION SECTION
# TEST 1

DIRECTIONS: Each question or incomplete statement is followed by several suggested answers or completions. Select the one the BEST answers the question or completes the statement. *PRINT THE LETTER OF THE CORRECT ANSWER IN THE SPACE AT THE RIGHT.*

1. Which of the following types of firewall techniques is most susceptible to IP spoofing?  1.____

    A. Proxy server
    B. Circuit-level gateway
    C. Packet filter
    D. Application gateway

2. Which of the following is a term for unorganized symbols, words, images, numbers or sound that a computer can transform into something useful?  2.____

    A. Software
    B. Data
    C. Input
    D. Information

3. In relational databases, records are referred to as  3.____

    A. stories
    B. tuples
    C. keys
    D. files

4. Web _____ can be included in HTML-formatted e-mail messages to reveal whether a recipient has received a message, as well as to disclose the recipient's IP address.  4.____

    A. cookies
    B. bots
    C. bugs
    D. tokens

5. Which of the following is NOT typically an element of a GUI?  5.____

    A. Column
    B. Icon
    C. Pointer
    D. Menu

6. Of the three general methods for posing queries to a database, choosing parameters from a menu  6.____

    A. is the least flexible
    B. is the most powerful
    C. requires the user to learn a specialized language
    D. presents the user with a blank record and lets him/her specify fields and values

7. Unless the circuitry is part of a workstation's design, LAN computers usually need a(n) _____ to function in the network.

    A. NIC
    B. bus
    C. protocol
    D. EDI

7.____

8. A VPN enables a business to

    A. avoid network "tear-downs"
    B. make use of the Internet, rather than build a dedicated network
    C. make a network inherently more secure
    D. work on circuits, rather than packets

8.____

9. In a client/server architecture, the component that performs the bulk of the data processing operations is known as the

    A. fat client
    B. portal
    C. server
    D. node

9.____

10. The process of translating virtual addresses into real addresses is known as

    A. paging
    B. ghosting
    C. mapping
    D. swapping

10.____

11. The first commercially developed operating system was

    A. OS1
    B. Windows
    C. OS360
    D. DOS

11.____

12. The relationships between cells in a spreadsheet application are known as

    A. formulas
    B. references
    C. attributes
    D. labels

12.____

13. Most contemporary personal computers come with external cache memory that sits between the CPU and the main memory. This cache is known as the _____ cache.

    A. disk
    B. DRAM
    C. Level 1 (L1)
    D. Level 2 (L2)

13.____

14. Only _____ language programs can manipulate CPU registers.   14.____
    I. machine
    II. assembly
    III. high-level
    IV. fourth-generation

    A. I and II
    B. II only
    C. I, II and III
    D. IV only

15. In the _____ process, the amplitude of an analog wave is checked at regular intervals in   15.____
    order to enable its encoding into digital form.

    A. attenuation
    B. sampling
    C. amplification
    D. modulation

16. In the _____ phase of the systems development life cycle, programmers either write   16.____
    software from scratch or purchase software from a vendor.

    A. implementation
    B. maintenance
    C. needs analysis
    D. development

17. The term "warm boot" refers to   17.____

    A. getting a quick view of stored files
    B. placing files in a more secure location
    C. restarting a computer that is already on
    D. making files more quickly available on a disk

18. In terms of digital security, nonrepudiation can be accomplished through each of the fol-   18.____
    lowing, EXCEPT

    A. confirmation services
    B. timestamps
    C. nym servers
    D. digital signatures

19. More advanced microprocessors may begin executing a second instruction before the   19.____
    first has been complete. This is a feature known as

    A. multitasking
    B. burst mode
    C. pipelining
    D. cascading

20. The main disadvantage associated with ATM network technology is that it

    A. tends to favor audio and video over traditional data
    B. creates cells of unpredictable size
    C. does not respond well to fluctuations in network traffic
    D. requires large startup costs

21. Computer users make use of hypertext in browser software by clicking the mouse on a

    A. graphic image
    B. pull-down menu choice
    C. hot spot
    D. button

22. Products using the IEEE 1394 interface may use each of the following names, EXCEPT

    A. i.link
    B. USB
    C. Fire Wire
    D. Lynx

23. What is the term for the computer's processing circuitry, located within the system's case?

    A. CPU
    B. RAM
    C. Motherboard
    D. BIOS

24. The primary difficulty in using a LAN to directly connect telephone calls to a server is that

    A. it would prevent the LAN from working with another remote network
    B. the configuration of the network would change into something that could not strictly be considered a "LAN"
    C. most LAN technologies don't handle voice data very well
    D. the link would require synchronous data

25. Graphical software developers can create virtual environments from two-dimensional images by making use of

    A. Quicktime VR
    B. MPEG
    C. transcoding
    D. Cinepak

26. In the design of an information system, a(n) _____ is often useful to show all organizations, departments, users, applications, and data that function in the system.

    A. Gantt chart
    B. data dictionary
    C. schema
    D. entity-relationship diagram

27. Which of the following terms is NOT synonymous with the others?

    A. Bit rate
    B. Vertical frequency
    C. Refresh rate
    D. Frame rate

28. What is the term for the process of adding depth to an image using a volumetric dataset (a set of cross-sectional images)?

    A. Voxelization
    B. Texelization
    C. Interpixellation
    D. Rounding out

29. Assembly language must be translated into _____ before it can run on a computer.

    A. source code
    B. pseudocode
    C. machine language
    D. BASIC

30. Indexing a database field offers the benefit of

    A. establishing an encryption code for selected data items
    B. allowing for the programming of an interface
    C. duplicating information contained within the field for backup purposes
    D. accelerating searches in that field

31. Some computer keyboards have a(n) _____ integrated into them, between the g and h keys.

    A. mini-mouse
    B. trackball
    C. light pen
    D. integrated pointing device

32. Which of the following is a 16-bit standard for denoting characters that can represent most of the world's languages?

    A. ANSI
    B. ASCII
    C. Unicode
    D. ISO Latin-1

33. Mosaic is a _____ browser.

    A. graphical
    B. text-only
    C. markup
    D. plug-in

34. Which of the following can be used to enhance the performance of executing commands on a database?

    A. Connection pools
    B. Two-phase commits
    C. Fixed lengths
    D. Triggers

35. The FIRST step in the photolithographic process is

    A. soft baking
    B. wafer cleaning
    C. barrier layer formation
    D. mask alignment

36. Computer program instructions
    I. are explicit and unequivocal
    II. perform only one task each
    III. are translated into binary code before execution
    IV. are executed in sequence

    A. I and II
    B. I, II and III
    C. III and IV
    D. I, II, III and IV

37. When transferred to a different computer, a(n) _____ language requires very little reprogramming.

    A. high-level
    B. machine
    C. assembly
    D. natural

38. Typically, the operating system kernel is responsible for managing each of the following, EXCEPT

    A. peripherals
    B. program execution
    C. memory
    D. disk

39. The UNIX operating system was the first major program written in the computer language

    A. Ada
    B. C
    C. Java
    D. C++

40. The _____ version of a software product is given to manufacturers to bundle into future versions of their hardware products.   40._____

    A. alpha
    B. maintenance
    C. crippled
    D. RTM

41. MOUS is an acronym that stands for   41._____

    A. Memory Overload/Unusable System
    B. Modulation User Set
    C. Microsoft Office Utility Service
    D. Microsoft Office User Specialist

42. The opposite of "time sharing" in microprocessing is   42._____

    A. multitasking
    B. autosizing
    C. multiprocessing
    D. batch processing

43. A standard compact disc can contain about _____ MB of data.   43._____

    A. 480
    B. 650
    C. 720
    D. 800

44. Which of the following is LEAST similar to the others in its function?   44._____

    A. Extension
    B. Command file
    C. Script
    D. Macro

45. Tools for analyzing data in spreadsheet programs include each of the following, EXCEPT   45._____

    A. conceptual problem-solving
    B. risk modeling
    C. sensitivity analysis
    D. goal seeking

46. Many optical scanners are capable of gray scaling, and typically use from _____ different shades of gray.   46._____

    A. 8 to 32
    B. 16 to 256
    C. 512 to 1024
    D. 300 to 600

47. A language that is designed to specify the layout of a document is known as a(n) _____ language.   47.____

   A. object-oriented
   B. query
   C. assembly
   D. markup

48. A hacker enters the computer system of his credit card company and changes a charge from $1,250.00 to $12.50. This is an example of the computer crime known as   48.____

   A. Van Eck bugging
   B. salami attack
   C. piggybacking
   D. data diddling

49. In the hexadecimal coding system, 1111 equals the   49.____

   A. number two
   B. number four
   C. letter D
   D. letter F

50. A URL may include information about   50.____
   I. what protocol to use
   II. the IP address
   III. the domain name
   IV. the type of file

   A. I and II
   B. II and III
   C. II, III and IV
   D. I, II, III and IV

## KEY (CORRECT ANSWERS)

| | | | | |
|---|---|---|---|---|
| 1. C | 11. C | 21. D | 31. D | 41. D |
| 2. B | 12. A | 22. B | 32. C | 42. D |
| 3. B | 13. D | 23. A | 33. C | 43. B |
| 4. C | 14. B | 24. C | 34. A | 44. A |
| 5. A | 15. B | 25. A | 35. B | 45. A |
| 6. A | 16. D | 26. D | 36. D | 46. B |
| 7. A | 17. C | 27. A | 37. A | 47. D |
| 8. B | 18. C | 28. A | 38. A | 48. D |
| 9. A | 19. C | 29. C | 39. B | 49. D |
| 10. C | 20. C | 30. D | 40. D | 50. D |

# TEST 2

DIRECTIONS: Each question or incomplete statement is followed by several suggested answers or completions. Select the one the BEST answers the question or completes the statement. *PRINT THE LETTER OF THE CORRECT ANSWER IN THE SPACE AT THE RIGHT.*

1. Because of their vertical arrangement, the OSI Reference Model and the TCP/IP protocols are referred to as network protocol

    A. towers
    B. stacks
    C. dunes
    D. compilers

    1.____

2. _____ of the operating system are less frequently used, and copied from the disk as needed.

    A. Nonresident
    B. Peripheral
    C. Application
    D. Unthreaded

    2.____

3. Presentation programs such as PowerPoint often use the _____ effect to blend slides together while switching from one to the next.

    A. dithering
    B. transition
    C. slumping
    D. fade-in

    3.____

4. In a network in which transactions are being recorded, the _____ strategy is designed to ensure that either all the databases on the network are updated or none of them, so that the databases remain synchronized.

    A. dynaset
    B. two-phase commit
    C. failover
    D. aggregate function

    4.____

5. Which of the following is an optical storage device?

    A. CD-ROM
    B. Floppy disk
    C. Hard disk
    D. Cassette tape

    5.____

6. The capacity of RAM is measured in

    A. bytes
    B. kilobytes
    C. megabytes
    D. gigabytes

    6.____

7. The four stages of the CPU's operation cycle, in sequence, are 7.\_\_\_\_

   A. execute, store, decode, fetch
   B. fetch, execute, translate, store
   C. fetch, decode, execute, store
   D. encode, store, decode, fetch

8. In a database application, a _____ check validation would ensure that a worker's salary did not exceed the maximum of $53,599. 8.\_\_\_\_

   A. range
   B. completeness
   C. sequence
   D. consistency

9. In a _____ network, all nodes have equivalent capabilities and responsibilities. 9.\_\_\_\_

   A. peer-to-peer
   B. file server
   C. frame relay
   D. client/server

10. Which of the following is NOT a common technology for the storage of binary information? 10.\_\_\_\_

    A. Analog
    B. Magnetic
    C. Optical
    D. Electronic

11. Typically, the term "legacy application" is applied to 11.\_\_\_\_

    A. productivity software
    B. newer, more innovative programs
    C. database management systems
    D. operating systems

12. Which of the following is NOT an example of a database application? 12.\_\_\_\_

    A. Parts inventory system
    B. Automated teller machine
    C. Mortgage calculator
    D. Flight reservations system

13. A computer component may signal the CPU that it has data available by 13.\_\_\_\_

    A. shorting the bus
    B. fetching an instruction
    C. flushing the pipeline
    D. sending an interrupt

14. The hexadecimal numbering system uses a base of

    A. eight
    B. twelve
    C. sixteen
    D. thirty-two

15. POSIX is

    A. a set of standards to make applications independent of the UNIX operating system
    B. an open-source alternative to the UNIX operating system
    C. a set of standards that makes an operating system look like UNIX to an application
    D. a specialized form of the UNIX operating system for use in medical/ health care applications

16. The type of programming language that most closely mirrors human ways of thinking is _____ language.

    A. assembly
    B. object-oriented
    C. translator
    D. query

17. The main reason hard disks are used to store data instead of much faster technologies, such as DRAM, is because hard disks are

    A. capable of reorganizing data from location to location
    B. less prone to read/write errors
    C. more amenable to recovery if something goes wrong
    D. not volatile

18. The final step in producing an executable program is to

    A. translate pseudocode into source code
    B. translate the source code into object code
    C. translate source code into a language such as C or FORTRAN
    D. transform the object code into machine language

19. What is the term for software that has been written into ROM?

    A. Warez
    B. Pseudocode
    C. Firmware
    D. Macrocode

20. Variables play an important role in computer programming because they enable programmers to

    A. maintain strict quality-control standards
    B. make programs backward compatible
    C. avoid repeated iterations
    D. write flexible programs

21. The foremost organization for information systems personnel and managers is the

    A. Data Processing Management Association
    B. United States Chief Information Officers Council
    C. Information Resources Management Association
    D. Association of Internet Professionals

22. Second-generation graphics systems improved upon first-generation systems by

    A. adding shading capabilities
    B. supporting texture-mapping
    C. allowing for the movement of objects in 3D space
    D. enabling full-scene antialiasing

23. Suitable standards for testing the quality of a computer program include each of the following, EXCEPT

    A. semantic errors
    B. logic errors
    C. robustness
    D. reliability

24. Bitmap file formats include each of the following, EXCEPT

    A. GIF
    B. CGM
    C. PNG
    D. DIB

25. The largest collection of information in a database is the

    A. file
    B. system
    C. field
    D. record

26. Of the telephone technologies listed below, the oldest is

    A. FDDI
    B. PSTN
    C. SONET
    D. ISDN

27. The primary difference between a "workstation" and a regular desktop system lies in

    A. graphics capabilities
    B. the operating system
    C. microprocessing speeds
    D. the number of users

28. In contemporary personal computers, the stripped-down operating system is stored in _____ before a computer is turned on.  28._____

    A. RAM
    B. ROM
    C. the hard disk
    D. the CPU

29. When a computer is multitasking, the _____ controls the flow of program tasks through the CPU.  29._____

    A. RAM
    B. CPU
    C. disk cache
    D. operating system

30. A digital pulse, viewed on an oscilloscope, appears as a  30._____

    A. square wave
    B. short dash
    C. microwave
    D. gamma wave

31. The first operating system developed with preemptive multitasking was  31._____

    A. MS-DOS
    B. OS/2
    C. Windows
    D. UNIX

32. Each of the following methods of data compression may involve temporal compression, EXCEPT  32._____

    A. JPEG
    B. Content-based
    C. MPEG
    D. P-frame

33. A network manager is considering the implementation of ATM technology. Because the organization uses the network primarily for file transfers, the most appropriate type of ATM service would be _____ bit rate.  33._____

    A. available
    B. variable
    C. constant
    D. unspecified

34. Which type of color model is typically used in commercial printing?  34._____

    A. CIE
    B. RGB
    C. HGB
    D. CMYK

35. The _____ is an allotted space in which spreadsheet programs allow users to create and edit data and formulas.

    A. register
    B. formula bar
    C. data field
    D. status bar

36. The four-layered protocol that was instrumental in the expansion of the Internet is

    A. OSI
    B. ATM
    C. TCP/IP
    D. UDP/IP

37. The most common top-level domain name suffix used on the World Wide Web is

    A. .gov
    B. .edu
    C. .org
    D. .com

38. The process of synchronizing databases that exist in different localities is known as

    A. replication
    B. distribution
    C. storehousing
    D. backup

39. Productivity software that uses a document-centric approach is made possible by the compound document standards known as

    A. XML and HTML
    B. VAP and AWT
    C. JFS and ISAM
    D. OLE and OpenDoc

40. What is the term for a WAN or LAN that uses TCP/IP protocols and can be accessed only by users from within the organization that owns the network?

    A. Extranet
    B. Intranet
    C. Supranet
    D. Isonet

41. File compression technologies that attempt to eliminate redundant or unnecessary information, such as the technology used with MPEG files, are described as

    A. terse
    B. DCT
    C. lossy
    D. stripped

42. What is the term for a database that is designed to help managers make strategic business decisions?

    A. Data mine
    B. Operational data store
    C. Data mart
    D. Data warehouse

43. Which type of computer virus exploits the automatic command execution capabilities of certain types of application software?

    A. Macro virus
    B. Worm
    C. Trojan horse
    D. Zombie

44. All computers use a _____ to translate between digital code and audio signals.

    A. sound card
    B. SMDI
    C. audio scrubber
    D. Sound Blaster

45. A hard disk's storage capacity can be increased by means of

    A. caching
    B. virtual memory
    C. boot blocking
    D. file compression

46. _____ a standard for describing the location of resources on the World Wide Web.

    A. FTP
    B. URL
    C. XML
    D. HTML

47. Which of the following is a multithreading operating system?

    A. UNIX
    B. MS-DOS
    C. VMS
    D. Linux

48. Probably the easiest method for committing computer crime today is

    A. shoulder surfing
    B. piggybacking
    C. Trojan horses
    D. below-threshold attacks

49. Which of the following types of servers enables users to log on to a host computer and perform tasks as if they're working on the remote computer itself?

    A. Middleware
    B. Telnet
    C. IRC
    D. FTP

50. _____ occurs when a programmer places source code and a compiler or interpreter on a different computer platform, and then creates working object code.

    A. Assembling
    B. Reconfiguring
    C. Replication
    D. Porting

## KEY (CORRECT ANSWERS)

| | | | | |
|---|---|---|---|---|
| 1. B | 11. C | 21. A | 31. D | 41. C |
| 2. A | 12. C | 22. A | 32. A | 42. C |
| 3. B | 13. D | 23. A | 33. D | 43. A |
| 4. B | 14. C | 24. B | 34. D | 44. A |
| 5. A | 15. C | 25. A | 35. B | 45. D |
| 6. A | 16. B | 26. B | 36. C | 46. B |
| 7. C | 17. D | 27. A | 37. D | 47. D |
| 8. A | 18. D | 28. B | 38. A | 48. A |
| 9. A | 19. C | 29. D | 39. D | 49. B |
| 10. A | 20. D | 30. A | 40. B | 50. D |

# EXAMINATION SECTION
## TEST 1

DIRECTIONS: Each question or incomplete statement is followed by several suggested answers or completions. Select the one that BEST answers the question or completes the statement. *PRINT THE LETTER OF THE CORRECT ANSWER IN THE SPACE AT THE RIGHT.*

1. The speed disparity between adjacent devices can cause problems with an interface. These problems are usually resolved by temporarily storing input in a(n)

    A. channel  
    B. control unit  
    C. register  
    D. buffer

    1.____

2. A typical computer spends most of its time

    A. compiling
    B. waiting for input or output
    C. executing instructions
    D. interpreting commands

    2.____

3. What is the basic input device on a small computer?

    A. Keyboard    B. Cursor    C. Mouse    D. Processor

    3.____

4. When two hardware devices want to communicate, they will FIRST exchange _____ signals.

    A. interrupt    B. protocol    C. interface    D. boot

    4.____

5. Which of the following is retrieved and executed by the processor?

    A. Instructions  
    B. Clock pulses  
    C. Information  
    D. Data

    5.____

6. What type of architecture is used by most microcomputers?

    A. Standard  
    B. Serial  
    C. Single-bus  
    D. Multiple-bus

    6.____

7. Typically, _____ is NOT a problem associated with a computer's main memory.

    A. cost  
    B. volatility  
    C. capacity  
    D. speed

    7.____

8. Which of the following types of memory management is the SIMPLEST?

    A. Sector-oriented  
    B. Dynamic  
    C. Block-oriented  
    D. Fixed partition

    8.____

9. What is the term for the time during which a disk drive is brought up to operating speed and the access device is positioned?

    A. E-time  
    B. Rotational delay  
    C. Seek time  
    D. Access time

    9.____

10. What type of code is written by programmers?

    A. Load module
    B. Source
    C. Object
    D. Operating

11. A _____ is the basic output device on a small computer.

    A. printer
    B. keyboard
    C. display screen
    D. hard disk

12. Which of the following serves to manage a computer's resources?

    A. User
    B. Operating system
    C. Programmer
    D. Software

13. A computer processes data into

    A. information
    B. pulses
    C. code
    D. facts

14. What is the term for the entity used to link external devices to a small computer system?

    A. Interface
    B. Network
    C. Plug-in
    D. Modem

15. For a transaction processing application, a _____ file organization should be selected.

    A. sequential
    B. indexed
    C. direct
    D. random

16. Which element of a microcomputer directly controls input and output?

    A. Buffer
    B. Processor
    C. Bus
    D. Control unit

17. A computer's data and program instructions are stored in

    A. memory
    B. the video buffer
    C. a program
    D. an output port

18. What is the term for the metal framework around which most microcomputers are constructed?

    A. Mainframe
    B. Hard disk
    C. Motherboard
    D. Expansion slot

19. The read/write head of a computer's disk drive is contained on the

    A. magnetic drum
    B. data element
    C. token
    D. access mechanism

20. A(n) _____ is used to link a small computer's secondary storage device to the system.

    A. control unit
    B. interface board
    C. register
    D. buffer

21. What processor management technique is used on most timesharing network systems?

    A. Time-slicing
    B. Command sorting
    C. Apportionment
    D. Interrupt processing

22. Which of the following procedures is used to copy data from a slow-speed device to a high-speed device for eventual input to a program?  22.____

    A. Queuing
    B. Spooling
    C. Buffing
    D. Scheduling

23. A location in memory is located by its  23.____

    A. section   B. register   C. address   D. decoder

24. _____ data is represented by a wave.  24.____

    A. Microwave   B. Digital   C. Binary   D. Analog

25. A programmer defines the logical structure of a problem by using a(n)  25.____

    A. assembler
    B. compiler
    C. interpreter
    D. nonprocedural language

## KEY (CORRECT ANSWERS)

1. D
2. B
3. A
4. B
5. A

6. C
7. D
8. D
9. C
10. B

11. C
12. B
13. A
14. A
15. C

16. B
17. A
18. C
19. D
20. B

21. A
22. B
23. C
24. D
25. D

# TEST 2

DIRECTIONS: Each question or incomplete statement is followed by several suggested answers or completions. Select the one that BEST answers the question or completes the statement. *PRINT THE LETTER OF THE CORRECT ANSWER IN THE SPACE AT THE RIGHT.*

1. Data is converted from digital to analog form through the process of  1.____
   - A. demodulation
   - B. teleporting
   - C. cross-modulation
   - D. modulation

2. Which of the following represents the simplest data structure?  2.____
   - A. Record
   - B. File
   - C. List
   - D. Directory

3. The term for a set of parallel wires used to transmit data, commands, or power is  3.____
   - A. bus
   - B. cabling
   - C. line
   - D. twisted pair

4. _____ limit the number of peripherals that can be linked to a microcomputer system.  4.____
   - A. Channels
   - B. Bus lines
   - C. Buffers
   - D. Slots

5. A data structure in which memory is allocated as a series of numbered cells is a(n)  5.____
   - A. array
   - B. block
   - C. record
   - D. register

6. On a disk, each program's name and location can be located on the  6.____
   - A. index
   - B. address
   - C. label
   - D. register

7. Onto which of the following structures is a processing chip stored?  7.____
   - A. Board
   - B. Plate
   - C. Bus
   - D. Disk

8. Two or more independent processors can share the same memory under a system known as  8.____
   - A. time-sharing
   - B. FAT binaries
   - C. multitasking
   - D. multiprocessing

9. A _____ is the basic storage unit around which a microcomputer system is designed.  9.____
   - A. bit
   - B. block
   - C. word
   - D. byte

10. A user communicates with an operating system by means of a(n)  10.____
    - A. interface
    - B. peripheral
    - C. command language
    - D. application

11. A _____ is used to convert data from pulse form to wave form and back again.  11.____
    - A. channel
    - B. modem
    - C. SCSI port
    - D. bus

12. Data values can be accessed according to their element numbers in a(n)  12.____
    - A. list
    - B. register
    - C. record
    - D. array

13. Under a _____ memory management scheme, a program is allocated as much memory as it needs.

    A. sector-oriented
    B. dynamic
    C. block-oriented
    D. fixed partition

14. What is the term for the process of removing errors from a program?

    A. Compiling
    B. Debugging
    C. Troubleshooting
    D. Extraction

15. _____ is the term for the time during which a desired sector of a disk approaches the access device.

    A. Run time
    B. Rotational delay
    C. Seek time
    D. Access time

16. What is the term for the process by which a networked computer selects the terminal it will communicate with?

    A. Compiling
    B. Polling
    C. Interfacing
    D. Selection

17. After compilers and assemblers read a programmer's code, they generate a(n)

    A. object module
    B. nonprocedural language
    C. subroutine
    D. load module

18. Memory that loses its content when the machine's power is turned off is described as

    A. read-only
    B. redundant
    C. dependent
    D. volatile

19. Which module of an operating system sends primitive commands to a disk drive?

    A. Motherboard
    B. IOCS
    C. CPU
    D. Command processor

20. The BASIC measure of data communications speed is

    A. bit rate
    B. baud rate
    C. kilobytes per second
    D. bits per second

21. The term _____ is used to denote a single, meaningful data element, such as a person's telephone number.

    A. field    B. item    C. record    D. file

22. What is the term for the machine-level translation of a programmer's source code?

    A. Load module
    B. Subroutine
    C. Source library
    D. Object module

23. Which part of an instruction directs the actions of the processor?

    A. Pulse
    B. Operation code
    C. Statement
    D. Operand

24. A _____ is used to store programs that enter a multiprogramming system.

    A. tape    B. spool    C. buffer    D. queue

25. _____ is a device used to avoid data dependency and redundancy.   25.\_\_\_\_

    A. Sequential filing  
    B. Continuous backup  
    C. Random filing  
    D. Database

---

# KEY (CORRECT ANSWERS)

1. A
2. C
3. A
4. D
5. A

6. A
7. A
8. D
9. C
10. C

11. B
12. D
13. B
14. B
15. B

16. B
17. A
18. D
19. B
20. B

21. A
22. D
23. B
24. D
25. D

# EXAMINATION SECTION
# TEST 1

DIRECTIONS: Each question or incomplete statement is followed by several suggested answers or completions. Select the one that BEST answers the question or completes the statement. *PRINT THE LETTER OF THE CORRECT ANSWER IN THE SPACE AT THE RIGHT.*

1. A track and a sector number on a disk combine to form a(n)   1.____

    A. register   B. byte   C. address   D. file name

2. A(n) _____ microcomputer system design focuses on what must be done, but not on how to do it.   2.____

    A. logical   B. listed   C. protocol   D. objective

3. An instruction is retrieved from main memory by the _____ processor component.   3.____

    A. arithmetic and logic unit   B. instruction counter
    C. register   D. instruction control unit

4. What is the term for a support program that reads a source program, translates the source statements to machine language, and outputs a complete binary object program?   4.____

    A. Scheduler   B. Interpreter   C. Compiler   D. Assembler

5. A(n) _____ is composed of a group of related data records.   5.____

    A. array   B. list   C. directory   D. file

6. What is the term for an extra bit added to data bits that will allow a computer to check the bit pattern for accuracy?   6.____

    A. End code   B. Bit stuffer
    C. Operand   D. Parity bit

7. When disks are stacked into a pack, what is the term for the set of tracks accessed by the access device?   7.____

    A. Block   B. Sector   C. Cylinder   D. Drum

8. Any data communications medium can be described by the generic term   8.____

    A. line   B. port   C. converter   D. modem

9. The operating systems of most microcomputers are driven by   9.____

    A. commands   B. hardware
    C. software   D. a control unit

10. What is the term for a complete machine-level program that is in a form ready to be placed into main memory and executed?   10.____

    A. Load module   B. Object module
    C. Schedule   D. Compiler

83

11. A programmer writes one instruction for each machine-level instruction when using a(n)   11.___

    A. generator          B. assembler
    C. resource fork      D. compiler

12. A binary digit is represented by a   12.___

    A. byte     B. code     C. bit     D. buffer

13. Which module of the operating system is responsible for communicating with input and output devices?   13.___

    A. Command processor    B. Boot
    C. IOCS                 D. Bus line

14. Two or more disks stacked on a common drive shaft are known as a   14.___

    A. pack         B. roll-out
    C. multidrive   D. cylinder

15. The _____ of an operating system loads programs into main memory.   15.___

    A. compiler     B. processor manager
    C. scheduler    D. assembler

16. A _____ can be used to synchronize devices or media that operate at different speeds.   16.___

    A. buffer   B. spooler   C. modem   D. protocol

17. The part of an instruction that identifies memory locations to participate in an operation is the   17.___

    A. pulse     B. statement
    C. operand   D. operation code

18. What is the term for a support program that reads a single source statement, translates the statement to machine language, executes the instructions, and then moves onto the next source statement?   18.___

    A. Scheduler   B. Interpreter
    C. Compiler    D. Assembler

19. _____ is used to link a computer's internal components.   19.___

    A. Cables         B. Bus lines
    C. Clock pulses   D. Motherboard

20. Data are transferred from main memory to a disk's surface in units called   20.___

    A. sectors   B. blocks   C. tracks   D. words

21. Under a _____ memory management scheme, programs are stored on disk, with only active portions stored into memory.   21.___

    A. virtual          B. dynamic
    C. block-oriented   D. fixed partition

22. A(n) _____ is composed of a group of related data fields.

    A. array    B. list    C. record    D. file

23. Which of the following serves to allocate a processor's time?

    A. User
    B. Bus
    C. Operating system
    D. Motherboard

24. On a disk, the address of the beginning of each program is stored on the

    A. tree    B. block    C. index    D. register

25. A program's steps are divided into units of

    A. code
    B. commands
    C. sectors
    D. instructions

## KEY (CORRECT ANSWERS)

1. C
2. A
3. D
4. C
5. D
6. D
7. C
8. A
9. A
10. A
11. B
12. C
13. C
14. A
15. C
16. A
17. C
18. B
19. B
20. A
21. A
22. C
23. C
24. C
25. D

# TEST 2

DIRECTIONS: Each question or incomplete statement is followed by several suggested answers or completions. Select the one that BEST answers the question or completes the statement. *PRINT THE LETTER OF THE CORRECT ANSWER IN THE SPACE AT THE RIGHT.*

1. The address of the next instruction to be executed is held in the _____ processor component.   1.____

   A. main memory
   B. register
   C. arithmetic and logic unit
   D. instruction control unit

2. What is the term for an electronic signal that is part of a protocol?   2.____

   A. Token   B. Reach   C. Chord   D. Pulse

3. Under _____ processing, data records are processed in the order in which they are recorded.   3.____

   A. continuous   B. consecutive
   C. serial   D. sequential

4. _____ processing is a computer application in which data are collected over time and then processed together.   4.____

   A. Transaction   B. Cumulative
   C. Batch   D. Continuous

5. A(n) _____ serves as a hardware/software interface.   5.____

   A. buffer   B. application
   C. operating system   D. bus

6. Any connection for an electronic communication line can be called a(n)   6.____

   A. port   B. poll   C. line   D. front end

7. During a single machine cycle, a processor retrieves and executes   7.____

   A. one command
   B. one instruction
   C. at least two statements
   D. at least two instructions

8. A _____ is NOT an example of a data structure.   8.____

   A. record   B. file   C. list   D. directory

9. Which of the following serves to translate a computer's internal codes and a peripheral device's external codes?   9.____

   A. Buffer   B. RAM
   C. Interface   D. Encoder/decoder

10. Which of the following is the memory management scheme MOST often used with time-shared systems?

    A. Pages
    B. Roll-in/roll-out
    C. Fixed partitions
    D. First-come/first-serve

11. When the same data are recorded in two or more files, _____ has occurred.

    A. redundancy
    B. leakage
    C. backup
    D. loss

12. For a batch processing application, a _____ file organization should be selected.

    A. sequential
    B. indexed
    C. direct
    D. random

13. If a bus line transmits bits one by one, it is described as a _____ line.

    A. serial
    B. consecutive
    C. continuous
    D. parallel

14. Data is converted from analog to digital form through the process of

    A. demodulation
    B. data flow
    C. cross-modulation
    D. modulation

15. A _____ loads a computer's operating system.

    A. program loader
    B. IOCS
    C. command processor
    D. boot

16. Which of the following differentiates a computer from a calculator?

    A. Memory
    B. Input
    C. A processor
    D. A stored program

17. Which element of a microcomputer system will devote a separate unit to suit each peripheral?

    A. Bus
    B. Channel
    C. Motherboard
    D. Interface

18. What is the term for the interference that distorts electronic signals transmitted over a distance?

    A. Ghosting
    B. Noise
    C. Static
    D. Interference

19. By responding to a(n) _____, an operating system can switch from program to program.

    A. operand
    B. user
    C. interrupter
    D. program

20. If a microcomputer system's memory capacity is adjusted, the result will be a change in

    A. word size
    B. processing speed
    C. precision
    D. seek time

21. A _____ generates the regular electronic pulses that drive a computer.

    A. clock   B. IOCS   C. bus   D. processor

22. Under what type of access can data records be accessed in any order?

    A. Serial
    C. Direct
    B. Random
    D. Sequential

23. A _____ is a brief message printed or displayed by a program or the operating system that asks the user for input.

    A. token   B. seek   C. protocol   D. prompt

24. Data on a disk are recorded in a series of concentric circles called

    A. blocks   B. tracks   C. cycles   D. sectors

25. What is the term for a programming language in which one mnemonic source statement is coded for each machine-level instruction?

    A. Scheduler
    C. Compiler
    B. Interpreter
    D. Assembler

## KEY (CORRECT ANSWERS)

1. B
2. A
3. D
4. C
5. C

6. A
7. B
8. D
9. C
10. B

11. A
12. A
13. A
14. D
15. D

16. D
17. D
18. B
19. C
20. B

21. A
22. C
23. D
24. B
25. D

# EXAMINATION SECTION

# TEST 1

DIRECTIONS: Each question or incomplete statement is followed by several suggested answers or completions. Select the one that BEST answers the question or completes the statement. *PRINT THE LETTER OF THE CORRECT ANSWER IN THE SPACE AT THE RIGHT.*

1. A spreadsheet program is NOT used for

   A. determining averages
   B. scheduling
   C. writing reports
   D. estimating job costs

   1.\_\_\_\_

2. In order to write-protect a 3.5" floppy disk, a user must

   A. cover the write-protect notch
   B. move the write-protect tab down, leaving an opening in the corner of the disk
   C. cover the recording window
   D. immobilize the shutter mechanism

   2.\_\_\_\_

3. Which of the following is a mathematical function of a spreadsheet program?

   A. Averages
   B. Logarithms
   C. Standard deviation
   D. Maximum/minimum values

   3.\_\_\_\_

4. The purpose of a device driver is to

   A. tell hardware devices precisely how to perform their jobs
   B. manage the movement of a read/write head over a hard disk drive
   C. facilitate the I/O interface
   D. manage the movement of a read/write head over a floppy disk

   4.\_\_\_\_

5. Each of the following is a purpose that is typically served with a desktop publishing program EXCEPT

   A. printing newsletters
   B. illustrating manuals
   C. creating flyers
   D. printing menus

   5.\_\_\_\_

6. Which of the following is an operating system that relies on icon selection or menu options to select commands?

   A. OS/2  B. Unix  C. MS-DOS  D. Windows

   6.\_\_\_\_

7. Typically, the quality of a printer is expressed in terms of

   7.\_\_\_\_

A. resolution
B. RAM
C. DPI
D. pixellation

8. Which of the following is a purpose that can be served by a database program?   8._____

    A. Balancing accounts
    B. Illustrating manuals
    C. Keeping track of schedules
    D. Generating client reports

9. What type of adapter would be required if a user wanted to upgrade the graphics capability of a computer monitor to a maximum number of 256 possible colors?   9._____

    A. XGA         B. CGA         C. VGA         D. SVG

10. Which of the following is a statistical function of a spreadsheet program?   10._____

    A. Maximum/minimum values
    B. Logarithms
    C. Absolute values
    D. Compounding periods

11. For which of the following functions would a flat-file database be MOST useful?   11._____

    A. Compiling invoices
    B. Creating a graph based on stored sales figures
    C. Storing information to print mailing labels
    D. Calculating inventory

12. Data in electronic spreadsheets are stored in areas called   12._____

    A. records
    B. cells
    C. plug-ins
    D. fields

13. If a user on a network wants to receive information from a host computer, he/she would have to _____ the desired files.   13._____

    A. uplink
    B. translate
    C. write a call program for
    D. download

14. A _____ is an optical storage device.   14._____

    A. video buffer
    B. floppy disk
    C. CD-ROM
    D. magnetic tape

15. Each of the following is a function served by a utility program EXCEPT　　15._____
    A. removing viruses
    B. setting alarms
    C. creating reports
    D. creating menus

Questions 16 through 25 concern the DOS command-driven environment. For the purpose stated next to each number, choose the command that would need to be typed next to the prompt on a user's computer screen.

16. To find out what's stored on a disk, type　　16._____
    A. ver    B. dir    C. list    D. cd

17. To clear the display screen, type　　17._____
    A. ren    B. chkdsk    C. clear    D. cls

18. To create a directory or subdirectory, type　　18._____
    A. md    B. rd    C. ren    D. new

19. To display the version number of the installed DOS, type　　19._____
    A. type    B. DOStype    C. format    D. ver

20. To delete a directory or subdirectory, type　　20._____
    A. del    B. md    C. rd    D. delete

21. To prepare a hard disk for formatting, type　　21._____
    A. format    B. fdisk    C. chkdisk    D. rd

22. To list the contents of an ASCII file on screen, type　　22._____
    A. file    B. list    C. type    D. asc

23. To copy a file or directory, type　　23._____
    A. xcopy    B. file/dir    C. copy    D. diskcopy

24. To rename a file, type　　24._____
    A. name    B. cd    C. rest    D. ren

25. To delete a directory, type　　25._____
    A. rmdir    B. cd    C. del    D. deldir

# KEY (CORRECT ANSWERS)

| | | | |
|---|---|---|---|
| 1. | C | 11. | C |
| 2. | B | 12. | B |
| 3. | B | 13. | D |
| 4. | A | 14. | C |
| 5. | B | 15. | C |
| 6. | A | 16. | B |
| 7. | C | 17. | D |
| 8. | D | 18. | A |
| 9. | D | 19. | D |
| 10. | A | 20. | C |

21. B
22. C
23. A
24. D
25. A

# TEST 2

DIRECTIONS: Each question or incomplete statement is followed by several suggested answers or completions. Select the one that BEST answers the question or completes the statement. *PRINT THE LETTER OF THE CORRECT ANSWER IN THE SPACE AT THE RIGHT.*

NOTE: The questions on this test concern Macintosh applications.

1. Mac users can find the amount of space available on a disk
    A. in the upper right-hand corner of the disk window
    B. by consulting the System file
    C. by keying command-M
    D. only by using the Get Info command under a File menu

2. The simplest way for a user to make a copy of a file into another folder on the same disk is to
    A. select the file, then choose *duplicate* from the file menu
    B. hold down the option key as the file is dragged into the folder
    C. select the file and press command-D
    D. make a copy onto a floppy disk and then drag that copy back onto the hard disk

3. When a user drags a file from the hard disk to a floppy disk, the user is
    A. moving the file from the hard disk to the floppy disk
    B. making a copy of the file for the hard disk
    C. making a copy of the file onto the floppy disk
    D. deleting the file

4. When printing to a new printer for the first time, which of the following should be performed FIRST?
    A. Choose the printer driver
    B. Choose the name of the printer
    C. Select *Chooser* from the Apple or File menu
    D. Click the setup button or choose Auto Setup

5. When using a mouse to select an icon, which of the following actions is necessary?
    A. Single-click
    B. Double-click
    C. Press
    D. Press and drag

6. When using a mouse to see what's in a menu, which of the following actions is necessary?
    A. Single-click
    B. Double-click
    C. Press
    D. Press and drag

7. When using a mouse to open a file, you should
    A. single-click
    B. double-click
    C. press
    D. press and drag

8. What is the keyboard shortcut for closing a window displayed on the desktop?

    A. Command-W
    B. Control-Option-E
    C. Command-C
    D. Command-O

9. When the *Save As* dialog box is on the desktop, what is the visual cue that the displayed list has been selected?

    A. All file names appear in gray
    B. A flashing insertion point
    C. Folder names appear in black
    D. A double border around the list

10. In any text environment, pressing the delete key will cause the_____ to back up a space.

    A. finder
    B. I-beam
    C. insertion point
    D. pointer

11. The keyboard shortcut for pasting text is Command-_____.

    A. V    B. X    C. B    D. C

12. Which control panel would be used to change the size of the type of the windows on the desktop?

    A. General Controls
    B. Views
    C. Monitors
    D. Labels

13. Which control panel would be adjusted to display fewer colors on the monitor in order to save memory?

    A. ColorSync
    B. Views
    C. Monitors
    D. Labels

14. If a real file is thrown away by a user, its aliases will

    A. remain unaffected
    B. be deleted also
    C. remain but may only provide access to text files
    D. remain on the disk but will not provide access to anything

15. In any set of buttons on the desktop, the default button will

    A. be bordered in gray
    B. be lettered in gray
    C. have a thick double border
    D. be lettered in black

16. Whenever a menu item is followed by an ellipsis (...), the selection of that item will produce a(n)

    A. opened file
    B. dialog box
    C. opened application
    D. choice among listed Control Panels

17. When a set of options appear with checkbox buttons next to them, this is a clue that

    A. a submenu will be produced by clicking a button
    B. any number of buttons may be selected or deselected in combination
    C. clicking a button will not produce any changes until the computer is restarted
    D. only one of the buttons may be selected at a time

18. If a disk's, folder's or application's icon appears gray, it is a sign that the item

    A. that created it cannot be found
    B. is about to have its name changed
    C. is already open
    D. has been deleted from the RAM

19. If a document icon is blank, it is probably a sign that

    A. it has already been opened
    B. the application that created it has already been opened
    C. it has been deleted
    D. the application that created the document cannot be found on the disk

20. If a scroll bar in a window or dialog box appears gray, it is a sign that

    A. there are other items in the window that are not currently visible
    B. the display needs vertical centering
    C. the scroll box is not available
    D. the display needs horizontal centering

21. What is the keyboard shortcut for creating a new folder?

    A. Command-W
    B. Command-F
    C. Command-N
    D. Control-Option-F

22. What is the visual clue that the name of a file, folder or disk on the desktop is about to be changed?

    A. A border has appeared around the name
    B. The entire icon is highlighted
    C. The name is highlighted
    D. The entire icon is gray

23. To print the contents of an entire screen, a user should

    A. choose *Print* from the file menu while running an application
    B. choose *Print Desktop* from the file menu

C. press Command-P
D. choose *Print Window* from the file menu

24. When the *Save As* dialog box is on the desktop, what should a user do to select the edit box for input?

    A. Press the Tab key
    B. Click on the *Save* button
    C. Press the Shift key
    D. Press Command-S

25. To put files back where they came from, a user should

    A. drag the file into the System folder while the *Fast Find* Apple menu is running
    B. press Command-W
    C. create an alias
    D. press Command-Y

# KEY (CORRECT ANSWERS)

1. A
2. B
3. C
4. C
5. A

6. C
7. B
8. A
9. D
10. C

11. A
12. B
13. C
14. D
15. C

16. B
17. B
18. C
19. D
20. A

21. C
22. A
23. B
24. A
25. D

# EXAMINATION SECTION
# TEST 1

DIRECTIONS: Each question or incomplete statement is followed by several suggested answers or completions. Select the one that BEST answers the question or completes the statement. *PRINT THE LETTER OF THE CORRECT ANSWER IN THE SPACE AT THE RIGHT.*

1. A disk error is caused by  1.____
   - A. slow processor
   - B. faulty RAM
   - C. settings issue of CMOS
   - D. all of the above

2. 10/100 in network interface means  2.____
   - A. protocol speed
   - B. mega bit per second
   - C. fiber speed
   - D. server speed

3. The tracks of hardware is subdivided as  3.____
   - A. vectors   B. disks   C. sectors   D. clusters

4. ESD damages the  4.____
   - A. power supply
   - B. expansion board
   - C. keyboard
   - D. monitor

5. On the I/O card, the _____ drive has the 34 pin.  5.____
   - A. floppy   B. SCSI   C. IDE   D. all of the above

6. In case of a failure of power supply, what kind of beep will you hear?  6.____
   - A. Short beep
   - B. One long beep
   - C. Continuous long beeps
   - D. All of the above

7. Which of the following adapters will you set before you install a SCSI CD-ROM?  7.____
   - A. An unused SCSI address
   - B. B0007
   - C. SCSI ID-1
   - D. None of the above

8. What would you use to evaluate the serial and parallel ports?  8.____
   - A. High volt probe
   - B. Cable scanner
   - C. Loop backs
   - D. Sniffer

9. An error message of 17xx means a problem with  9.____
   - A. CMOS
   - B. ROM BIOS
   - C. DMA control
   - D. hard drive

10. The bi-directional bus is called a _____ bus.  10.____
    - A. data   B. control   C. address   D. multiplexed

11. _____ defines the quality of the printer output.
    A. Dot per inch
    B. Dot per square inch
    C. Dots printed per unit time
    D. Dots pixel

12. What would you do if APM stops functioning?
    A. Uncheck "enable advanced printing feature"
    B. Check "print spooled documents first"
    C. Check "start printing after last page"
    D. All of the above

13. What would you do to import XML incorporating GUID to a tally?
    A. Transfer data into MS Excel sheet and import to tally account
    B. Import Export Menu
    C. Both A and B
    D. None of the above

14. The writing device for the Palm is called a
    A. stylus
    B. pointer
    C. cursor
    D. none of the above

15. A USB port of a computer has the ability to connect _____ number of devices.
    A. 12
    B. 154
    C. 127
    D. 8

16. A _____ problem causes a system to not boot and beep.
    A. motherboard
    B. RAM
    C. BIOS
    D. hard disk

17. What would you do if the computer cannot access the website in the corporate setting?
    A. Take a look at the proxy server
    B. Check user authentication
    C. Ping Hosts
    D. Check firewall

18. Which of the following is used to measure the database size?
    A. The total disk space
    B. Select sum (bytes)/1024/1024 from dba_data_files
    C. Both A and B
    D. None of the above

19. RAID defines
    A. fault tolerance
    B. data transfer rate
    C. random access memory
    D. read AID

20. The hard disk is measured in
    A. GHz
    B. GB
    C. Gigawatts
    D. MB

21. _____ cannot be shared over a network.
    A. Floppy
    B. Keyword
    C. Printer
    D. CPU

22. Access does not support
    A. number  B. picture  C. memo  D. text

23. A network map shows
    A. devices and computers on network
    B. the location of your computer on the network
    C. information about the network
    D. none of the above

24. While making a chart in MS Word, the categories are shown on
    A. X axis                B. Y axis
    C. none of the above     D. both A and B

25. What would you do if Google Chrome does not open on a corporate computer?
    A. Turn off the antivirus temporarily   B. Check date settings of computer
    C. Check settings of antivirus          D. All of the above

# KEY (CORRECT ANSWERS)

1. D
2. B
3. C
4. B
5. A

6. D
7. A
8. C
9. D
10. A

11. B
12. D
13. C
14. A
15. C

16. B
17. A
18. C
19. A
20. B

21. D
22. B
23. A
24. D
25. D

# TEST 2

DIRECTIONS: Each question or incomplete statement is followed by several suggested answers or completions. Select the one that BEST answers the question or completes the statement. *PRINT THE LETTER OF THE CORRECT ANSWER IN THE SPACE AT THE RIGHT.*

1. _____ is the computer's default IP address.
   A. 192.168.1.1 B. 255.000.1
   C. 01010101 D. None of the above

2. Which of the following is a scheduling algorithm?
   A. FCFS B. SJF
   C. RR D. All of the above

3. The trouble with the Shortest Job First algorithm is
   A. too long to be an effective algorithm
   B. to evaluate the next CPU request
   C. too complex
   D. all of the above

4. ADSL contains _____ as the largest bandwidth.
   A. voice communication B. upstream data
   C. downstream data D. control data

5. A Toshiba satellite ST1313 running Windows XP has trouble playing sounds. What would you do?
   A. Download sound driver for Realtek
   B. Install default Windows Vista
   C. Change sound card
   D. Change the speaker

6. What would you do if your Wi-Fi keeps disconnecting?
   A. Check to see if computer is in the range of Wi-Fi
   B. Install the latest PC wireless card
   C. Click troubleshoot problems
   D. All of the above

7. If your attachment in an e-mail is not opening, what is the problem?
   A. You don't have the software to open the file
   B. Your computer clock is at fault
   C. Your software is not compatible with the OS
   D. All of the above

8. A DIMM has _____ number of pins.
   A. 72 B. 32 C. 32 to 72 D. 71

9. What is the frequency of the SDRAM clock?  9._____
   A. 122 Mhz    B. 133 Mhz    C. 82 Mhz    D. 122 Ghz

10. IRQ6 is connected to  10._____
    A. sound card    B. Com1    C. floppy    D. LPT1

11. You can check the availability of the IRQ while installing PCI NICS through  11._____
    A. dip switches              B. CONFIG.SYS
    C. jumper setting            D. BIOS

12. What would you use if you have a smudged keyboard?  12._____
    A. TMC solvent               B. Silicone spray
    C. Alcohol                   D. All-purpose cleaner

13. Which port would you switch to if the laser printer is working slow?  13._____
    A. RS232    B. SCSI    C. Serial    D. Parallel

14. If a mouse is moving erratically, the problem is  14._____
    A. dirty ball                B. faulty connection
    C. faulty driver             D. faulty IRQ setting

15. If a dot matrix printer quality is light, it is an issue of  15._____
    A. paper quality             B. faulty ribbon advancement
    C. head position             D. low cartridge

16. When configuring the hard drive, what would you do after low-level format?  16._____
    A. Formatting the DOS partition    B. Install OS
    C. Hard disk partition             D. None of the above

17. Which of the following errors means a change in two or more bits of data?  17._____
    A. Burst                     B. Double bit
    C. Single bit                D. All of the above

18. Pentium system voltage is _____ volts.  18._____
    A. +12    B. +5    C. +8    D. +3.3

19. What would you do if the IDE hard drive is not recognized by the system after installation?  19._____
    A. Install drivers                    B. Check the jumpers on hard disk
    C. Check information of hard disk     D. All of the above

20. What would you do to abort a deadlock?  20._____
    A. Terminate deadlock process
    B. Terminate the programs one by one
    C. Terminate programs at once
    D. All of the above

21. What would you do if you cannot share files over the network? 21._____
    A. Check network discovery
    B. Check Share files
    C. Check password protection
    D. All of the above

22. How would you protect a corporate computer from losing data due to a utility power blackout? 22._____
    A. Install a surge protector
    B. Install uninterrupted power supply
    C. Reduce power consumption
    D. All of the above

23. What would you do if the network key is lost? 23._____
    A. Install the latest network
    B. Clear cache
    C. Set up the router again
    D. None of the above

24. What settings prevent issues if you forget the password to log into Windows? 24._____
    A. Check use account and family safety
    B. Boot in to install disk and rest password
    C. Both A and B
    D. None of the above

25. What would you do to troubleshoot a computer monitor? 25._____
    A. Turn off the power supply
    B. Hold down the power button
    C. Check settings of the monitor
    D. All of the above

## KEY (CORRECT ANSWERS)

| | | | |
|---|---|---|---|
| 1. | A | 11. | D |
| 2. | D | 12. | D |
| 3. | B | 13. | D |
| 4. | A | 14. | A |
| 5. | A | 15. | B |
| 6. | D | 16. | A |
| 7. | A | 17. | A |
| 8. | A | 18. | D |
| 9. | B | 19. | B |
| 10. | C | 20. | C |

| | |
|---|---|
| 21. | D |
| 22. | D |
| 23. | C |
| 24. | A |
| 25. | B |

# TEST 3

DIRECTIONS: Each question or incomplete statement is followed by several suggested answers or completions. Select the one that BEST answers the question or completes the statement. *PRINT THE LETTER OF THE CORRECT ANSWER IN THE SPACE AT THE RIGHT.*

1. What would you do if your monitor has no display while it is getting power? 1.____
   A. Check picture settings
   B. Switch to a functional monitor
   C. Check video card
   D. All of the above

2. How would you troubleshoot DirectX? 2.____
   A. Install DirectX diagnostic tool
   B. Run troubleshoot
   C. Re-install DirectX
   D. All of the above

3. What would you do if there is a conflict of network IP address? 3.____
   A. Convert Static IP address to DHCP
   B. Exclude Static IP address from DHCP server
   C. Both A and B
   D. None of the above

4. _____ defines the time interval between process submission and completion. 4.____
   A. Waiting time
   B. Turnaround time
   C. Response time
   D. Throughput

5. Mutual exclusion _____ for a non-sharable device including printers. 5.____
   A. must exist
   B. must not exist
   C. may exist
   D. may not exist

6. A kernel cannot schedule 6.____
   A. kernel level thread
   B. user level thread
   C. process
   D. all of the above

7. What would you do if the computer is not able to find the C: drive when you boot? 7.____
   A. Swap hard drives to identify the issue
   B. Reboot
   C. Put your hard drive in a bag and place it in a freezer for the night
   D. All of the above

8. Data security does not need a 8.____
   A. big RAM
   B. strong password
   C. audit log
   D. scan

9. What would you do if you get an error message that prompts, "Cannot obtain IP"?
   A. Open command prompt
   B. Type "ipconfig/renew" in the command prompt
   C. Click the troubleshoot network
   D. All of the above

10. _____ should be used to transfer large data.
    A. DMA
    B. Programmed I/O
    C. Controller register
    D. LPT1

11. What would you do after recovery from a system failure?
    A. Repair ingeneration of the system
    B. Notify the parties at both ends
    C. Adjust the recovery system
    D. Systematically log failures

12. _____ is not present in a computer.
    A. USB port
    B. Parallel port
    C. ROM
    D. Com1/Com2

13. _____ produces a print with pins of grid.
    A. Inkjet
    B. Laser
    C. Daisy wheel
    D. Dot matrix

14. What would you do if Windows Vista/7/XP does not sleep?
    A. Check settings of the device manager
    B. Uncheck all the options that wakes up the computer
    C. Look for advanced power management
    D. All of the above

15. What is the use of the System File Checker tool?
    A. Replace missing files
    B. Replace corrupt files
    C. Scan drive
    D. All of the above

16. What would you do if the PC reboots between the processes of updating?
    A. Undo updates by System Restore
    B. Go to recovery options
    C. Press F8 and select "repair your computer"
    D. All of the above

17. What would you do if there is no sound in a PC?
    A. Verify the settings
    B. Select default in Playback
    C. Check speaker cables
    D. All of the above

18. _____ keeps a record of the major events such as warning and errors.
    A. Event viewer
    B. Windows
    C. Windows Vista
    D. ALU

19. A run time error "DLL is not supported" means  19.____
    A. bad installation  B. corrupt MS Word
    C. low memory  D. all of the above

20. What would you do if the system gives error MSGSRV32 after  20.____
    recovering from power?
    A. Disable all programs using SETI  B. Disable power management
    C. Reboot computer  D. All of the above

21. While encrypting Windows XP files, you see "Encrypt contents to secure  21.____
    data" as grey. What is the possible reason?
    A. Using Windows XP home edition
    B. The hard drive is not NTFS formatted
    C. The hard drive is FAT32 file system
    D. All of the above

22. You get _____ error message if you are installing a program from a CD  22.____
    that is not clean.
    A. Win 32 application  B. Is not a valid Win 32 application
    C. Missing File Win 32  D. None of the above

23. What does it mean when the printer is blinking?  23.____
    A. Printer error  B. Printer ready
    C. Printer is processing  D. Printer is working

24. If MCI CD audio driver is not installed, the computer will  24.____
    A. not play audio CDs  B. mute DVD
    C. both A and B  D. none of the above

25. What would you do if the computer plug is emitting sparks?  25.____
    A. Disconnect all peripheral devices from the computer
    B. Change the power cord
    C. Check the power supply
    D. All of the above

## KEY (CORRECT ANSWERS)

1. D
2. A
3. C
4. B
5. A

6. B
7. D
8. A
9. B
10. A

11. A
12. D
13. D
14. D
15. D

16. D
17. D
18. A
19. A
20. A

21. D
22. B
23. A
24. A
25. D

# TEST 4

DIRECTIONS: Each question or incomplete statement is followed by several suggested answers or completions. Select the one that BEST answers the question or completes the statement. *PRINT THE LETTER OF THE CORRECT ANSWER IN THE SPACE AT THE RIGHT.*

1. How would you find out the APM version of Windows?  1.____
   A. Device Manager tab in the systems
   B. Install Advanced Power Management
   C. Check settings of control panel
   D. All of the above

2. How would you find the AMI POST beep codes?  2.____
   A. On the beep code page  B. On the CPU
   C. Settings  D. All of the above

3. MemTest86 is a _____ diagnostic tool.  3.____
   A. USB  B. bootable
   C. ineffective  D. all of the above

4. If you experience slow performance of your computer, the problem is  4.____
   A. RAM  B. processor  C. ROM  D. Throughput

5. How do you remove a RAM module?  5.____
   A. Pressing the small levers at both ends of the module
   B. Click safely remove hardware
   C. You cannot remove a RAM
   D. By uninstalling the RAM

6. How do you connect the computer clock with the Internet?  6.____
   A. By installing an Internet clock
   B. By setting the date in Time option in the control panel
   C. Processing the clock
   D. All of the above

7. To remove and re-install the real-time clock, you have to run the system on  7.____
   A. power  B. safe mode
   C. normal mode  D. all of the above

8. To keep track of the time, a computer has a battery called  8.____
   A. CMOS  B. CMAS  C. CMSC  D. CDMA

9. What is the problem if the graphic card is heating?  9.____
   A. Faulty motherboard  B. Driver issues
   C. Outdated BIOS  D. Faulty fan

10. What should you know or do before removing a failed PC power supply?
    A. ESD procedures
    B. Disconnect all connectors
    C. Both A and B
    D. None of the above

11. _____ drive has the faster data transfer rate.
    A. IDE
    B. SSD
    C. SATA
    D. Flash

12. SATA and IDE are two different types of ports used to connect
    A. storage devices
    B. RAM
    C. ROM
    D. graphic memory

13. Which of the following mediums cannot be used to install OS?
    A. CD/DVD ROM
    B. USB flash drive
    C. Floppy disk
    D. RAM

14. Which Windows is touch optimized?
    A. Windows ME
    B. Windows 8
    C. Windows Vista
    D. Windows 98

15. What is the other name used for a USB flash drive?
    A. Pen Drive
    B. Thumb Drive
    C. Flash Disk
    D. All of the above

16. RATS is defined as
    A. Regression Analysis Time Series
    B. Regression Analysis Time Sharing
    C. Real Analysis Series
    D. Real Analysis Time Series

17. _____ keeps a record of the major events such as warning and errors.
    A. Event viewer
    B. Windows
    C. Windows Vista
    D. ALU

18. You must use a _____ to notify Windows that you are about to uninstall Plug and Play devices.
    A. Device Manager
    B. Device Driver
    C. Control Panel
    D. Both A and B

19. _____ is used for data entry storage but not for processing.
    A. Mouse
    B. Dumb Terminal
    C. Micro computer
    D. Dedicated data entry system

20. Which of the following is NOT a PnP device?
    A. Mouse
    B. Printer
    C. Keyboard
    D. Joystick

21. WindowsKey + R takes you to
    A. Run
    B. Device Manager
    C. Hardware components
    D. None of the above

22. Which of the following has no dipswitches?  22.____
    A. Zorro Device              B. Micro channel
    C. NuBus                     D. All of the above

23. Use _____ to ensure security holes are patched.  23.____
    A. automatic updates         B. password
    C. both A and B              D. none of the above

24. What would you do if the speaker is not working?  24.____
    A. Check connectors          B. Check power supply
    C. Check sound card          D. All of the above

25. You get a message abclink.xyz when starting your computer. What would you do?  25.____
    A. Press any key to continue  B. Check settings
    C. Uninstall a program        D. All of the above

---

## KEY (CORRECT ANSWERS)

| | | | | |
|---|---|---|---|---|
| 1. | A | | 11. | B |
| 2. | A | | 12. | A |
| 3. | B | | 13. | D |
| 4. | A | | 14. | B |
| 5. | A | | 15. | D |
| 6. | B | | 16. | A |
| 7. | C | | 17. | A |
| 8. | A | | 18. | A |
| 9. | D | | 19. | B |
| 10. | C | | 20. | B |

21. A
22. A
23. A
24. D
25. D

# EXAMINATION SECTION
## TEST 1

DIRECTIONS: Each question or incomplete statement is followed by several suggested answers or completions. Select the one that BEST answers the question or completes the statement. *PRINT THE LETTER OF THE CORRECT ANSWER IN THE SPACE AT THE RIGHT.*

1. _____ is the data that has been organized or presented in a meaningful fashion.  1._____
   A. A process    B. Software    C. Storage    D. Information

2. Of the following data processing functions, which one is NOT a data processing function of a computer?  2._____
   A. Data gathering
   B. Processing data into information
   C. Analyzing the data or information
   D. Storing the data or information

3. In electronic data processing systems, which standard data code is used commonly to represent alphabetical, numerical and punctuation characters?  3._____
   A. ASCII    B. EBCDIC    C. BCD    D. All of the above

4. Data processing performed by several separate computers/networks, at several different locations, linked by a communications facility is known as _____ processing.  4._____
   A. distributed    B. centralized    C. on-line    D. batch

5. Which process is utilized by large retailers to study market trends?  5._____
   A. Data conversion    B. Data mining
   C. Data selection    D. Pos

6. In normalization, second normal form (2NF) eliminates in Tables  6._____
   A. all hidden dependencies
   B. the possibility of insertion anomalies
   C. all non-key fields depend on the whole primary key
   D. none of the above

7. Which of the following is a bottom-up approach for database design which is designed by examining the relationship between attributes?  7._____
   A. Functional dependency    B. Normalization
   C. Decomposition    D. None of the above

8. Which is the process that is used to restore data that has been stored in a computer?  8._____
   A. Retrieve    B. Backup    C. Recovery    D. Deadlock

9. Which term BEST explains the homogenous data type?
   A. Data items of same length
   B. Data items of same type
   C. Data items of different length
   D. Numerical and character date items

10. For any category of data being processed and any type of device used for this purpose, all data processing systems perform the same steps. Which is the CORRECT sequence?
    A. Analyzing, coding and execution
    B. Input, processing and output
    C. Input, organizing and processing
    D. Processing, storage and distribution

11. Which of the following e-data processing methods works on data that is accumulated from more than location and records that are updated instantly?
    A. Minicomputer system  B. Batch processing system
    C. On-line, real-time system  D. Micro computer system

12. Suppose you are employed by the Air Transport Company to design a database for an airline transaction system. The database has to capture the detailed level of data related to the tickets booked by the user and the updating made by them with timestamp. Which database model would be your preference?
    A. Dimensional model
    B. It can be either dimensional model or on-line transaction processing model
    C. On-line transaction processing model
    D. None of the above

13. In the database management system, what are the after triggers functions?
    A. Triggers generated after a particular operation
    B. Triggers run after an insert, update or delete on a table
    C. Triggers run after an insert, views, update or delete on a table
    D. None of the above

14. For trigger creation, a CREATE TRIGGER statement is used. So, clause _____ specifies the table name on which the trigger is to be attached. Also, _____ specifies that it is an AFTER INSERT trigger.
    A. for insert; on      B. on; for insert
    C. for; insert         D. none of the above

15. Which part of a data flow diagram (DFD) represents the people and organizations that send data that the system being modeled uses or produces?
    A. Processes    B. Data source    C. Data store    D. Data flow

16. The purpose of cryptography is
    A. deadlock removal       B. job scheduling
    C. protection             D. file management

17. _____ memory allocation method suffers from external fragmentation.
    A. Segmentation              B. Demand paging
    C. Swapping                  D. Paging

18. When working with a time-sharing operating system, when the time slot given to a process is completed, the process goes from the running state to the _____ state.
    A. blocked        B. ready        C. complete        D. terminated

19. The purpose of real-time systems
    A. is primarily used on mainframe computers
    B. monitors events instantly as they occur
    C. is employed in program development
    D. none of the above

20. What are the causes of process termination?
    A. Process is removed from all queues and process's PCB is de-allocated
    B. Process is completed
    C. Process control block is never de-allocated
    D. None of the above

21. Fragmentation of the file system
    A. occurs only if the file system is used improperly
    B. can always be prevented
    C. can be temporarily removed by compaction
    D. is a characteristic of all file systems

22. _____ scheduling is most suitable for a time-shared interactive system. It assigns the CPU to the first process in the ready queue for q time units. After q time units, if the process is not handed over to the CPU, it is blocked, and the process is put at the tail of the ready queue (done).
    A. Shortest-job-first (SJF)         B. CPU
    C. Round-robin (RR)                 D. None of the above

23. Backup can BEST be explained as
    A. a tool that must be offered by Windows operating system like Windows XP and 7 that checks when your system hardware and software need a new OS
    B. copy files from a computer to another medium, such as tape, DVD, another hard drive, or a removable drive
    C. a term that is used to move from one operating system to another, which may or may not involve implementing a new computer
    D. none of the above

24. As a Technical Support Officer for a large organization, at times you have to deal with login authentication problems of user computers. Which of the following is NOT a best practice for password policy?
    A. Restriction on password reuse
    B. Password encryption
    C. Having changed passwords every two years
    D. Deciding maximum age of password
    E. None of the above

25. When working in a team environment, the BEST adopted problem-solving technique in which all members of a team fully accept and support a decision is
    A. compromise
    B. goal
    C. consensus
    D. none of the above

## KEY (CORRECT ANSWERS)

| | | | | |
|---|---|---|---|---|
| 1. | D | | 11. | C |
| 2. | C | | 12. | C |
| 3. | A | | 13. | B |
| 4. | A | | 14. | B |
| 5. | B | | 15. | B |
| 6. | A | | 16. | C |
| 7. | B | | 17. | A |
| 8. | A | | 18. | B |
| 9. | B | | 19. | B |
| 10. | B | | 20. | A |

21. A
22. C
23. B
24. C
25. C

# TEST 2

DIRECTIONS: Each question or incomplete statement is followed by several suggested answers or completions. Select the one that BEST answers the question or completes the statement. *PRINT THE LETTER OF THE CORRECT ANSWER IN THE SPACE AT THE RIGHT.*

1. A collection of facts like drawings, pictures and stock figures is called
   A. quantity
   B. product
   C. data
   D. collector's item
   E. information

   1.____

2. The electronic data processing technique that collects data into groups to permit convenient and efficient processing is known as
   A. document-count processing
   B. batch-processing
   C. generalized-audit processing
   D. multiprogramming

   2.____

3. Lee runs a grocery store; he wants to keep a record of daily sold items. Lee uses a bar chart for this purpose to show many breads he sold per day. Each day has its own bar. How could he find the total number of breads sold?
   A. Finding the height of the tallest bar
   B. Adding together the heights of all the bars in the chart
   C. Counting the number of bars
   D. Finding the average of the values of each bar

   3.____

4. A summary level view of a system and the highest-level DFD is provided to the reader with the help of
   A. data store
   B. data source
   C. context diagram
   D. documentation

   4.____

5. Which option BEST explains the *triggers*?
   A. A statement that enables the start of any DBMS
   B. A statement that is executed by the user when debugging an application program
   C. A statement that is executed automatically by the system as a side effect of modification to the database
   D. None of the above

   5.____

6. Virtual memory technique is implemented with the help of
   A. segmentation
   B. fragmentation
   C. paging
   D. none of the above

   6.____

7. Which diagram is used to represent the relationship between the input, processing and output of an AIS?
   A. Flowchart
   B. Data flow diagram
   C. Document flowchart
   D. System flowcharts

   7.____

8. _____ scheduling is the simplest scheduling technique that forces the short processes to wait for very long processes.
   A. Round-robin (RR)
   B. Last-in, first out (LIFO)
   C. Shortest-job-first (SJF)
   D. First-come, first-served (FCFS)

9. Mapping of file is managed by
   A. paging table
   B. virtual memory
   C. file system
   D. file metadata

10. On-line analytical processing is also called _____ processing.
    A. decision support
    B. on-line transactional
    C. transaction control
    D. none of the above

11. When working in large organizations, you have to deal with different access authentication situations. To ensure security, you have multiple options in such conditions. Which of the following is the LEAST secure method of authentication for your organization?
    A. Key card
    B. Fingerprint
    C. Retina pattern
    D. Password

12. DML stands for
    A. data management language
    B. data markup language
    C. data manipulation language
    D. none of the above

13. Which term BEST explains the characteristics of a computer to run several operations simultaneously?
    A. Concurrency   B. Deadlock   C. Backup   D. Recovery

14. In DBMS, what is the BEST way to represent the attributes in a large database?
    A. Relational-and
    B. Concatenation
    C. Dot representation
    D. All of the above

15. Database locking mechanism is used to rectify the problem of
    A. lost update
    B. uncommitted dependency
    C. inconsistent data
    D. none of the above

16. In the scheme (dept name, size), we have relations (total inst 2010, total inst 2013). Which dependency has led to this relation?
    A. Company name, year->size
    B. Year->size
    C. Company name->size
    D. Size->year

17. Which is the BEST possible option to evaluate any scheduling algorithm?
    A. CPU utilization
    B. Throughput
    C. Waiting time
    D. All of the above

18. When the round robin CPU scheduling technique is adopted in a time-shared system,
    A. very large time slice degenerates into first-come, first-served algorithm
    B. extremely small time slices improve performance
    C. extremely small time slices degenerates into LIFO algorithm
    D. medium sized time slices leads to shortest request time first algorithm

19. A priority scheduling BIGGEST issue is
    A. definite blocking            B. starvation
    C. priority queues              D. none of the above

20. 

    The above figure is called a(n) _____ in use case diagram.
    A. person                       B. substitute
    C. actor (symbol)               D. flow directive

21. Use case models can be summed up into
    A. use case diagram             B. use case description
    C. all of the above             D. none of the above

22. Prototype
    A. is a working model of different parts at different levels or all of a final product
    B. does not represent any sort of models
    C. can never consist of full size
    D. all of the above

23. Kim has been given some official documents to type. While typing, he notices that some of the words are automatically changing. He is very interested to understand the purpose of this feature in MS Word. AutoCorrect is designed to replace _____ words as you type.
    A. short, repetitive            B. grammatically incorrect
    C. misspelled                   D. none of the above

24. As a computer associate, you have to write different reports like weekly departmental updates and specially designed tasks to analyze the different areas of an organization. Of the following, which is considered good reporting practices?
    A. Report factual observations, not opinions
    B. Identify proper personnel
    C. Formalize your inspection criteria
    D. None of the above

25. To improve the competency of teams, members of a(n) _____ team have been cross-trained so that each person is capable of performing the duties of all the other team members.  25.____
    A. functional
    B. cross-functional
    C. multifunctional
    D. self-directed

## KEY (CORRECT ANSWERS)

1. C
2. B
3. B
4. C
5. C

6. C
7. D
8. C
9. D
10. A

11. D
12. C
13. A
14. B
15. C

16. A
17. D
18. A
19. B
20. C

21. C
22. A
23. C
24. A
25. D

# TEST 3

DIRECTIONS: Each question or incomplete statement is followed by several suggested answers or completions. Select the one that BEST answers the question or completes the statement. *PRINT THE LETTER OF THE CORRECT ANSWER IN THE SPACE AT THE RIGHT.*

1. Information is _____ unfinished data.  1._____
   A. always  B. not  C. occasionally  D. none of these

2. Which option BEST explains Beta software?  2._____
   A. An early development version of software in which there are likely to be bugs.
   B. Software will expire in 30 days after its download.
   C. Software that has successfully passed the alpha test stage.
   D. Up-gradation of software is not possible.

3. Jane drew a bar chart to show the number of different cars he saw daily on his way back home. There was no bar above the Mercedes. What does this mean?  3._____
   A. He did not see any Mercedes during his trip
   B. No Mercedes exist in his city
   C. He selected a wrong type of chart
   D. He has never seen a Mercedes before

4. A flowchart is a picture representation of a program. Flows should initiate from top to bottom and from right to left. This flowcharting principle is commonly known as the _____ rule.  4._____
   A. narrative  B. sandwich  C. direction  D. consistency

5. The database designing approach which is based on a bottom-up approach that is designed by examining the relationship between attributes is  5._____
   A. functional dependency  B. database modeling
   C. normalization  D. decomposition

6. In an operating system, a situation occurs in which one process is in a waiting queue on another process that is also waiting on another process and the last one is waiting on the first process so no process is progressing in this waiting circular. This is called  6._____
   A. deadlock  B. starvation
   C. dormant  D. none of the above

7. Which access control method is considered the BEST approach for restricting system access to authorized users?  7._____
   A. Role-based access control  B. Process-based access control
   C. Job-based access control  D. None of the above

8. Which of the following is a disadvantage of a distributed system?  8._____
   A. Incremental growth  B. Reliability
   C. Resource sharing  D. All of the above

9. Which of the following is the BEST example of batch processing?
   A. Video game control
   B. Online reservation system
   C. Preparing pay bills of employees
   D. None of the above

10. Which of the following techniques was initiated to keep both CPU and the I/O devices busy because it was not possible with the single job?
    A. Time-sharing
    B. Spooling
    C. Preemptive scheduling
    D. Multiprogramming

11. Distributed operating system is based on the principle of
    A. single system image
    B. multi-system image
    C. wireless networks
    D. none of the above

12. The following components are helpful in a successful database environment EXCEPT
    A. users
    B. database
    C. separate files
    D. database administrator

13. In DBMS, which of the following is NOT schema?
    A. Database schema
    B. Logical schema
    C. None of the above

14. Of the following, which SQL Query is used to remove the table and all its data from the database?
    A. Drop table
    B. Delete table
    C. Alter table
    D. None of the above

15. *Ellipses* in DBMS means
    A. weak entity set
    B. attributes
    C. primary key
    D. none of the above

16. The method which performs a set of union of two "similarly structured" tables is called
    A. union
    B. join
    C. addition
    D. none of the above

17. All details about the files, its ownership, permissions, and location of file contents are stored in
    A. file control block (FCB)
    B. computer history
    C. file system
    D. none of the above

18. The drawback of a file management system to store data is
    A. data redundancy and inconstancy
    B. difficulty in accessing data
    C. data isolation
    D. all of the above

19. Which of the following is a feature of the machine independent operating system?
    A. Management of real time memory
    B. File processing
    C. I/O supervision
    D. Job scheduling
    E. B and D
    F. A and C

20. As a computer support officer, you are given details for your company's customers, consisting of two lists of names and addresses. You need to produce it in an individual document that consists of both names and address list. For this purpose, which mail merge would you prefer?
    A. Main document
    B. Data source
    C. Mail merge
    D. Merge field

21. After once creating a customer list with mail merge, which button will help you to add, delete or update your customer list?
    A. *Data Source* button
    B. *Edit* button
    C. *Edit Data Source* button
    D. *Data Editing* button

22. Which of the following steps is NOT a part of the three basic *Mail Merge Helper* steps?
    A. Merge the two files
    B. Create the main document
    C. Set the mailing list parameters
    D. Create the data source

23. As a computer support officer, while completing your assigned document typed in MS Word 2013, you need to insert the page number in the footer, but when you click on the insert tab > footer, it appears as *1*, but you wish to show *i* (roman numbers). What procedure will be followed?
    A. From Home, select bullets and numbering and configure the necessary setting
    B. From Insert Tab, choose Page Number and specify necessary setting
    C. Click on Page Number Icon and select Format Page Number and specify required setting
    D. All of the above

24. The problem statement contains the _____, which consists of these lists:
    I.   Lists specific input programs
    II.  Precise output values
    III. Perfect program would return for those input values

    A. Testing plan
    B. Error handler
    C. Requirement list
    D. Input-output specification

25. As a computer support officer who knows the stages of team development that will lead this team to a winning combination, what are the stages in proper sequence?
    A. Forming, storming, norming and performing
    B. Forming, norming, performing and finalizing
    C. Forming, storming, norming and playing
    D. None of the above

## KEY (CORRECT ANSWERS)

1. B
2. C
3. A
4. C
5. C

6. A
7. A
8. B
9. C
10. D

11. B
12. C
13. B
14. C
15. B

16. A
17. A
18. D
19. E
20. C

21. C
22. C
23. C
24. A
25. A

# TEST 4

DIRECTIONS: Each question or incomplete statement is followed by several suggested answers or completions. Select the one that BEST answers the question or completes the statement. *PRINT THE LETTER OF THE CORRECT ANSWER IN THE SPACE AT THE RIGHT.*

1. Data users are those who 1.____
   A. use data for their own advantage, breaking the law
   B. store files and data for their specific purposes
   C. use the data in databases
   D. none of the above

2. Which type of chart would be the BEST choice for showing how the temperature of a pizza changes over time when it is put in the oven? 2.____
   A. Pie chart          B. Line graph
   C. Bar chart          D. None of the above

3. As a computer support officer, you have to continuously update and organize your directories, folders and files on your computer. Which of the following BEST suits your requirement? 3.____
   A. Microsoft Word          B. Any spreadsheet application
   C. Windows Explorer        D. Microsoft Internet Explorer

4. Upgrade installation means 4.____
   A. preparation for installation, installation itself, any required or optional steps following the installation
   B. completely formatting the operating system on hardware and install new software
   C. type of system installation on a computer that already has an earlier version of the operating system
   D. none of the above

5. The main job of an operating system is 5.____
   A. command resources       B. manage resources
   C. provide utilities       D. none of the above

6. The MOST common source of change data in refreshing a data warehouse is _____ change data. 6.____
   A. queryable     B. cooperative     C. logged     D. snapshot

7. Which of the following is NOT an advantage of multiprogramming? 7.____
   A. Increased throughput
   B. Shorter response time
   C. Decreased operating system overhead
   D. Ability to assign priorities to jobs

8. In ERD, the rectangles are divided into two parts that show
   A. entity set
   B. relationship set
   C. set of attributes
   D. primary key

9. The MAXIMUM numbers of entities that can be participating in a relationship are designed with
   A. minimum cardinality
   B. maximum cardinality
   C. entity relation diagram
   D. none of the above

10. Which of the following is a multi-valued attribute?
    A. Phone number
    B. Name
    C. Date of birth
    D. Place of birth
    E. None of the above

11. Which term is used to refer to a specific record in your medicine database; for instance, information stored about a specific illness?
    A. Relation
    B. Instance
    C. Table
    D. None of the above

12. The relation stud (ID, name, house no., credit, house no., city, department) is decomposed into stud1 (ID, name)   stud2 (name, house no., city, department).  This type of decomposition is called
    A. lossless decomposition
    B. lossless-join decomposition
    C. both A and B
    D. none of the above

13. As a technical support officer for a large organization, you have to ensure the uninterrupted availability of data by creating backup to deal with every possible data loss.  Backup is taken by
    A. erasing all previous records and creating new records
    B. sending all log records from primary site to the remote backup site
    C. sending only selected records from main site to the alternate site
    D. none of the above

14. Verbal exchange of information between parents and a school staff when a student is moved from one department to another is a report which includes necessary information to maintain a consistent support for students of one department to another.  This report is known as a
    A. transfer report
    B. hand-off report
    C. graphic record
    D. report

15. Which portable storage device would you prefer for backups or showing your photographs to your friend?
    A. USB stick
    B. Hard drive
    C. Joystick
    D. None of the above

16. Which is the exact step for problem solving?
    A. Observe, evaluate and adjust
    B. Collect and analyze data
    C. Identify and analyze the problem
    D. Consider possible solutions

17. The software that maintains the time of a microprocessor to assure that all time critical events are processed as efficiently as possible and also system activities are divided into independent tasks is known as
    A. shell processor
    B. kernel
    C. device driver
    D. none of the above

18. Which of the following is the MOST appropriate scheduling technique in real time operating systems?
    A. Round robin
    B. FCFS
    C. Pre-emptive scheduling
    D. Random scheduling

19. Use case diagrams consist of
    A. actor
    B. prototype
    C. none of the above
    D. all of the above

20. Data warehouse means
    A. the actual directory of a knowledge
    B. the stage of selecting the right data for a KDD process
    C. a subject-oriented integrated time variant non-volatile collection of data in support of management
    D. all of the above

21. Jane wants to advertise her home-based bakery. For this purpose she needs to develop a two-column promotion for the daily local newspaper. She selected MS Word for this purpose, but does not know exactly which option to use. Of the following, what would you suggest she use for newspaper style columns?
    A. Insert Tab > Smart Art
    B. Table > Insert Table
    C. Insert Tab > Textbox
    D. Page Layout Tab > Columns

22. Of the following, what would you suggest Jane in Question 21 use to add Shimmer and Sparkle text in her advertisement to make it more attractive and eye capturing?
    A. Word Art
    B. Font styles
    C. Text effects
    D. Font effects

23. In MS Word, which indent marker is specific to control all the lines excluding the first line?
    A. First Line Indent Marker
    B. Left Indent Marker
    C. Hanging Indent Marker
    D. Right Indent Marker

24. When working as a computer support officer, you receive a help call from one of the users. The problem is that the user has just deleted an entire folder of important office notes. He needs to retrieve the data. Which method would you adopt to retrieve the contents?
    A. Empty the recycle bin
    B. Restore the folder from the recycle bin
    C. Once deleted, its contents cannot be retrieved
    D. No need to worry. Only the folder has been deleted, not its contents.

25. Documentation can be explained as
    A. a procedure used to provide technical information to specific audiences who have specific needs for that information
    B. an explanation about all procedures and their mechanisms
    C. a method that specifies the author, source and related detail about information
    D. none of the above

## KEY (CORRECT ANSWERS)

| | | | |
|---|---|---|---|
| 1. | B | 11. | A |
| 2. | B | 12. | D |
| 3. | C | 13. | B |
| 4. | C | 14. | A |
| 5. | B | 15. | A |
| 6. | E | 16. | C |
| 7. | C | 17. | B |
| 8. | A | 18. | C |
| 9. | B | 19. | D |
| 10. | A | 20. | C |

21. D
22. D
23. B
24. B
25. C

# EXAMINATION SECTION
## TEST 1

DIRECTIONS: Each question or incomplete statement is followed by several suggested answers or completions. Select the one that BEST answers the question or completes the statement. *PRINT THE LETTER OF THE CORRECT ANSWER IN THE SPACE AT THE RIGHT.*

1. When deciding the means by which training is to be delivered, the designer of instruction should FIRST select the  1.____

    A. type of delivery system technology
    B. trainer
    C. necessary instructional properties
    D. delivery system

2. _____ does NOT directly involve instruction, but offers the power to make learning more efficient.  2.____

    A. Computer-managed instruction (CMI)
    B. Computer-based training (CBT)
    C. Technical training function (TTF)
    D. Computer-assisted instruction (CAI)

3. The use of case studies as a means of instructional delivery should be avoided when  3.____

    A. training involves management or supervisory personnel
    B. instructional goals include critical thinking
    C. there is unhealthy competition among trainees
    D. time constraints on preparation exist

4. Each of the following is a function of audience response systems (ARS) software EXCEPT  4.____

    A. analyzing group responses to items
    B. performing demographic analyses
    C. storing scores for later analysis
    D. administering progressive evaluations during instruction

5. Which of the following is a step typically involved in the design phase of instructional design?  5.____

    A. Pilot instruction
    B. Developing instructional materials
    C. Analyzing job tasks
    D. Developing testing strategies

6. Which of the following is NOT a typical component of a performance support system (PSS)?  6.____

    A. Expert system
    B. Printed job aids
    C. Text retrieval
    D. Computer-aided instruction

7. An expert system includes knowledge structured for capturing regularly occurring circumstances. This structured knowledge is known as

   A. logic
   B. frames
   C. neural network processing
   D. rules

8. In a training situation, a(n) _____ is MOST likely to be held liable for misrepresentation.

   A. employer
   B. outside contractors/vendors
   C. owner/employer
   D. trainer

9. A good computer-assisted instruction delivery system will use

   A. norming
   B. scrolling
   C. page-turning
   D. branching

10. Each of the following is usually considered to be a characteristic of effective instructional design EXCEPT

    A. rule-based design
    B. holistic self-evaluation
    C. interconnected tasks
    D. systematic approach

11. Instructional media are typically used to

    A. direct learning activities
    B. predict the best method of instructional delivery
    C. support learning activities
    D. evaluate trainee performance

12. Which of the following instructional delivery techniques typically involves the LOWEST development cost?

    A. Audiotape
    B. Multimedia computer
    C. Lecture
    D. Live video

13. Computer-aided instruction is often designed so that only the precise knowledge needed at that point in the activity is taught.
    This is referred to as _____ CAI.

    A. secular
    B. granular
    C. partitioned
    D. modular

14. Each of the following is an advantage associated with the use of vendors as trainers EXCEPT

    A. no additional strain on training budget
    B. initiation of function that can later be turned over to in-house trainer
    C. usual offering of continued support
    D. proficiency in using new equipment or machines

15. Which of the following is a mode of computer-supported learning resources?

    A. Evaluation
    B. Tutorial
    C. Instructional games
    D. Hypermedia

16. Which of the following conditions does NOT typically indicate the use of performance support devices?

    A. Regulation requirements
    B. Frequently changing tasks
    C. Infrequently performed tasks
    D. Cost of mistakes is relatively low

17. Which of the following performance support devices can MOST accurately be described as *procedural*?

    A. Printed job aids
    B. Computer-based references (CBR)
    C. Hypertext
    D. Computer help systems

18. If a typical instructor-led training delivery system requires ten hours of instructional time, a textual computer-based training approach will typically require about _____ instructional hours.

    A. 40
    B. 100
    C. 200
    D. 400

19. Which of the following is an advantage associated with the use of performance observation as a means of gathering data during instructional design?

    A. Immediate response availability
    B. Minimal disturbance in work routines
    C. Generation of motivational information
    D. Low relative cost

20. Each of the following is a mode of computer-managed instruction EXCEPT

    A. record keeping
    B. simulation
    C. prescription generation
    D. testing

21. Which of the following is typically addressed in the evaluation strategy produced during instructional design?

    A. Balance of activities encompassed by the design
    B. Development of instructional materials
    C. Outcomes required to satisfy each performance criterion
    D. Provision of learner reinforcement

22. As a means of instructional delivery, role playing is useful under each of the following conditions EXCEPT when

    A. training involves the application of content knowledge
    B. technical or psychomotor skills are the focus
    C. training involves management or supervisory personnel
    D. instructional objectives are concerned with interpersonal relations

23. _____ is NOT a step typically involved in the analysis phase of instructional design.

   A. Writing instructional objectives
   B. Selecting tasks for training
   C. Determining instructional prerequisites
   D. Assessing learning requirements

24. Instruction delivered to new employees before they begin regular work is called _____ training.

   A. OJT
   B. vestibule
   C. independent study
   D. apprenticeship

25. If a company decides to contract out to an external training provider, each of the following elements must be included in a request for proposal EXCEPT

   A. project background
   B. outputs and deliverables
   C. delivery strategy
   D. project procedures

## KEY (CORRECT ANSWERS)

| | | | |
|---|---|---|---|
| 1. | C | 11. | C |
| 2. | A | 12. | C |
| 3. | D | 13. | B |
| 4. | D | 14. | B |
| 5. | D | 15. | D |
| 6. | B | 16. | D |
| 7. | B | 17. | A |
| 8. | B | 18. | C |
| 9. | D | 19. | B |
| 10. | B | 20. | B |

| | |
|---|---|
| 21. | C |
| 22. | B |
| 23. | C |
| 24. | B |
| 25. | C |

# TEST 2

DIRECTIONS: Each question or incomplete statement is followed by several suggested answers or completions. Select the one that BEST answers the question or completes the statement. *PRINT THE LETTER OF THE CORRECT ANSWER IN THE SPACE AT THE RIGHT.*

1. It is a good idea to use lecturing as a method of instructional delivery when

    A. complex processes need to be explained
    B. introducing training provided by other methods or media
    C. the trainer is unfamiliar with the audience
    D. instructional goals deal with affective or psycho-motor skills

2. Typically, the LARGEST part of all training costs is

    A. job aids
    B. vendor contracts
    C. travel expense associated with off-site training
    D. trainee salary during training

3. The systemic approach to training evaluation is typically divided into four parts. Which of the following is NOT one of these parts?

    A. Identification of trainee prerequisites
    B. Identification of training goals
    C. Production of learning outcomes
    D. Support performance development

4. During the instructional design process, an analysis document is produced which includes specifications for each of the following EXCEPT

    A. measurement factors
    B. target audience characteristics
    C. instructional media
    D. program management

5. Each of the following is a disadvantage associated with the use of employee-trainers EXCEPT

    A. least economical for recurrent training needs
    B. increased head count in labor budget
    C. less likely to have knowledge of adult learning techniques
    D. lack of knowledge of new-hire trainers

6. Which of the following is NOT among the modes of computer-assisted instruction?

    A. Problem solving          B. Calculation
    C. Modeling                 D. Drill and practice

7. Which of the following performance support devices offers the GREATEST availability to trainees?

    A. Printed job aids         B. Expert systems
    C. Hypertext                D. Computer help systems

8. Demonstrations might be used as a method of instructional delivery when
   A. instructional goals involve cognitive or affective domains
   B. dealing with especially large groups of trainees
   C. tasks require manual dexterity or are difficult for learners to understand
   D. when materials and equipment are scarce

9. Which of the following is typically addressed during the implementation phase of instructional design?
   A. Revision of instructional materials
   B. Selection of tasks for training
   C. Creation of design syllabus
   D. Creation of delivery strategy

10. The psychomotor domain of learning progresses in four discrete stages. Which of the following stages is typically the LAST to be accomplished?
    A. Manipulation
    B. Articulation
    C. Imitation
    D. Precision

11. A well-written instructional objective should include three key components. Which of the following is NOT one of these?
    A. Conditions
    B. Performance
    C. Media
    D. Criteria

12. If a job requires high technical knowledge but low manual skill, which of the following learning methods would be BEST suited for job training?
    A. Self-study and lab
    B. Classroom and on-the-job training with mentor
    C. Classroom and lab
    D. Classroom and self-practice

13. The computer- _____ component of technology-based training does NOT actually teach or manage instruction, but serves to make learning easier and more appropriate.
    A. managed instruction (CMI)
    B. based training (CBT)
    C. supported learning resource (CSLR)
    D. assisted instruction (CAI)

14. _____ simulation is used in information systems training.
    A. Manual
    B. Hybrid
    C. Sequential
    D. Computer

15. In order for trainees to move nonsequentially through a computerized training document, _____ will need to be installed.
    A. an expert system
    B. hypertext
    C. an authoring system
    D. a hierarchy

16. If a job requires high technical knowledge and manual skill, which of the following learning methods would be BEST suited for job training?

    A. Self-study and lab
    B. Classroom and on-the-job training with mentor
    C. Classroom and lab
    D. Classroom and self-practice

17. Which of the following is typically addressed in the design syllabus created during instructional design?

    A. Sequence in which content is presented
    B. Evaluation of training objectives
    C. Means of administering precourse assessment
    D. Evaluation of prerequisite skills

18. The use of peer tutoring as a method of instructional delivery will usually have all of the following benefits EXCEPT

    A. facilitating pacing of instruction in groups with heterogeneous abilities
    B. encouraging competition among trainees
    C. easing trainer"s workload
    D. increasing trainee's satisfaction with instruction

19. Which of the following instructional delivery techniques typically offers the GREATEST opportunity for self-pacing?

    A. Audiotape                B. Multimedia computer
    C. Lecture                  D. Live video

20. In the development of technology-based training, the logical starting point is computer-

    A. managed instruction (CMI)
    B. based training (CBT)
    C. supported learning resources (CSLR)
    D. assisted instruction (CAI)

21. As a means of instructional delivery, case studies are MOST useful for

    A. very large groups of trainees
    B. bridging theory and practice
    C. shaping attitudinal objectives
    D. drill and practice of psychomotor skills

22. An advantage commonly associated with the use of consultants as trainers is

    A. employees may be able to earn college credit for training course
    B. no increase in labor budget
    C. availability for modular training
    D. *one-shot* training

23. Discussion should be avoided as a method of instructional delivery when

    A. dealing with a group of trainees that is forty or larger
    B. content is rigid and restricted to facts
    C. there are strict time constraints on instruction
    D. instructional goals deal with attitudes or critical thinking skills

24. The component of technology-based learning that actually teaches is

    A. computer-managed instruction (CMI)
    B. computer-based training (CBT)
    C. technical training function (TTF)
    D. computer-assisted instruction (CAI)

25. Which of the following instructional delivery approaches would typically require the FEWEST number of development hours?

    A. Textual computer-based training
    B. Workbook
    C. Videotape
    D. Instructor-led

## KEY (CORRECT ANSWERS)

| | | | |
|---|---|---|---|
| 1. | B | 11. | C |
| 2. | D | 12. | D |
| 3. | A | 13. | C |
| 4. | C | 14. | D |
| 5. | A | 15. | B |
| 6. | B | 16. | B |
| 7. | A | 17. | A |
| 8. | C | 18. | B |
| 9. | A | 19. | B |
| 10. | B | 20. | A |

| | |
|---|---|
| 21. | B |
| 22. | B |
| 23. | C |
| 24. | D |
| 25. | D |

# EXAMINATION SECTION

## TEST 1

DIRECTIONS: Each question or incomplete statement is followed by several suggested answers or completions. Select the one that BEST answers the question or completes the statement. *PRINT THE LETTER OF THE CORRECT ANSWER IN THE SPACE AT THE RIGHT.*

1. The primary storage is
   A. used by processor
   B. used by RAM
   C. both A and B
   D. none of the above

   1.____

2. Clock speed is measured in
   A. hertz
   B. megahertz
   C. gigahertz
   D. none of the above

   2.____

3. Which of the following temperatures can cause component failure?
   A. 180 degrees   B. 185 degrees   C. 190 degrees   D. 205 degrees

   3.____

4. A motherboard has _____ connections to the power supply.
   A. one or more
   B. just one
   C. two
   D. none of the above

   4.____

5. CMOS setup is used
   A. to change motherboard settings
   B. for basic input/output
   C. both A and B
   D. none of the above

   5.____

6. ROM chips that can be overwritten are known as
   A. flash ROM
   B. micro ROM
   C. BIOS
   D. none of the above

   6.____

7. A secure way of transferring files from one device to another is
   A. FTP
   B. TFTP
   C. SFTP
   D. none of the above

   7.____

8. A method to provide access to a VPN is
   A. RAS   B. PPP   C. PPTP   D. IGP

   8.____

9. A big advantage of having a wireless standard is
   A. interoperability between devices
   B. greater device security
   C. both A and B
   D. none of the above

   9.____

10. When you are implementing a basic wireless network,
    A. disable ESSID broadcast
    B. don't configure the ESSID point
    C. both A and B
    D. none of the above

    10.____

11. You are installing a device that can throttle and detect peer-to-peer traffic. This device belongs to the device type
    A. load balancer
    B. bandwidth shaper
    C. proxy server
    D. none of the above

11._____

12. The first step involved in troubleshooting after arriving on the site is
    A. identifying the symptoms and drawing a network diagram
    B. comparing wiring schematics to the industry standards
    C. both A and B
    D. none of the above

12._____

13. _____ describes an email that has web links to direct users to malicious websites.
    A. Phishing
    B. Viruses
    C. Both A and B
    D. None of the above

13._____

14. You are troubleshooting network connectivity and want to see the path that the packets are taking from a workstation to the server. The _____ command line tool will be used for this.
    A. ping
    B. traceroute
    C. route
    D. nslookup

14._____

15. The process or steps required to be applied to develop an information system is
    A. system development life cycle
    B. program specification
    C. design cycle
    D. analytical code

15._____

16. Project plan is a document
    A. describing how the project team will develop the proposed system
    B. that outlines the technical feasibility of the proposed system
    C. both A and B
    D. none of the above

16._____

17. The primary goal of a system analyst is to
    A. create value for the organization
    B. create a wonderful system
    C. acquire a working tool
    D. none of the above

17._____

18. Understanding the purpose of the information system to be built and finding out how the project team is to accomplish making it is part of the _____ phase of the SDLC.
    A. analysis
    B. system request
    C. planning
    D. none of the above

18._____

19. Examining the economic, technical and organizational advantages and disadvantages of developing a new system is known as
    A. feasibility analysis
    B. committee approval
    C. risk analysis
    D. system request

19._____

20. The calculation measuring the amount of money an organization is going to get in return for the money it has spent is known as
    A. cash flow
    B. return on investment
    C. tangible costs
    D. none of the above

    20.____

21. New users should be encouraged to use software by taking help first from
    A. tutorial software
    B. training software
    C. both A and B
    D. none of the above

    21.____

22. A wizard is
    A. a person who can do magic
    B. software that helps and walks user through a complex process
    C. hardware that speeds up performance
    D. all of the above

    22.____

23. How can you determine the level of a trainee's knowledge?
    A. By watching them type
    B. By taking a test
    C. By asking them questions
    D. Both B and C

    23.____

24. Which of the following is the most important step when giving training users?
    A. Make them want to learn
    B. Push them until they master the task
    C. Leave learning or not learning up to them; just provide the training
    D. None of the above

    24.____

25. It is important that while training, the trainees are shown the
    A. training agenda
    B. results of previous training sessions
    C. trainer's achievements
    D. none of the above

    25.____

## KEY (CORRECT ANSWERS)

| | | | |
|---|---|---|---|
| 1. | C | 11. | B |
| 2. | A | 12. | A |
| 3. | B | 13. | A |
| 4. | A | 14. | B |
| 5. | A | 15. | A |
| | | | |
| 6. | A | 16. | A |
| 7. | C | 17. | A |
| 8. | C | 18. | C |
| 9. | A | 19. | A |
| 10. | A | 20. | B |

21. C
22. B
23. C
24. A
25. A

# TEST 2

DIRECTIONS: Each question or incomplete statement is followed by several suggested answers or completions. Select the one that BEST answers the question or completes the statement. *PRINT THE LETTER OF THE CORRECT ANSWER IN THE SPACE AT THE RIGHT.*

1. _____ makes it possible for the system to power up with the help of a keyboard.  
   A. ACPI  
   B. APM  
   C. Both A and B  
   D. None of the above  
   1._____

2. Which of the following are data path sizes?  
   A. 8, 16   B. 32, 64   C. 128   D. All of the above  
   2._____

3. The lines that carry the data in a bus is known as  
   A. data bus  
   B. memory bus  
   C. micro bus  
   D. none of the above  
   3._____

4. Which of the following can be used to boot, recover or reinstall the Windows operating system?  
   A. Recovery CD  
   B. Windows CD  
   C. Memory CD  
   D. None of the above  
   4._____

5. Which of the following explains the proper handling of substances like chemical solvents?  
   A. Material safety data sheet  
   B. POST  
   C. Memory data sheet  
   D. None of the above  
   5._____

6. A _____ tests a USB, networks, serial or other port.  
   A. loop back plug  
   B. three-head plug  
   C. both A and B  
   D. none of the above  
   6._____

7. Bundling network cables can cause  
   A. crosstalk  
   B. attenuation  
   C. collision  
   D. none of the above  
   7._____

8. The greatest concern while using an orbital satellite WAN link is  
   A. cable length   B. duplex   C. latency   D. collision  
   8._____

9. If packets to an IP address are dropping over the Internet, _____ will be used to determine the responsible hop.  
   A. netstat  
   B. traceroute  
   C. ping  
   D. none of the above  
   9._____

10. _____ ports can be used for FTP traffic.  
    A. 25   B. 24   C. 23   D. 20  
    10._____

139

11. The _____ connects multiple workstations, functions as a router and supports VLANs.
    A. hub
    B. multilayer switch
    C. switch
    D. repeater

12. To provide VoIP phones with power but without having to arrange independent power supplies for them, the switches on the network should have
    A. spanning tree
    B. PoE
    C. PPPoE
    D. VLAN tagging

13. _____ has the same functionality as Telnet but operates more securely.
    A. SSH
    B. RSH
    C. TFTP
    D. SNAT

14. You use a logical network diagram to determine the number of
    A. cables in the network
    B. broadcast domains on the network
    C. users on the network
    D. none of the above

15. Planning and controlling the system development within a deadline at the lowest cost and with the right functionality is called
    A. project management
    B. task identification
    C. task
    D. none of the above

16. One way of calculating project completion time is to apply industry standard factors for each phase of the project. In this method, the planning phase takes almost 15% of the total time. If a project takes three months for planning, then the remaining project will need approximately
    A. 20 months
    B. 15 months
    C. 3 months
    D. none of the above

17. Fourteen factors impact the complexity of a project when we are using a function point estimation worksheet. _____ are included in these factors.
    A. Data communications, end user efficiency and reusability
    B. Data communications, estimated effort and time tradeoffs
    C. Both A and B
    D. None of the above

18. In determining the tasks for a work plan, you can
    A. list the four phases of SDLC and steps occurring in each phase
    B. control and direct the project
    C. establish a possible reporting structure
    D. none of the above

19. If someone is examining existing paperwork so that he can better understand the As-Is system, this is
    A. observation
    B. JAD
    C. document analysis
    D. none of the above

20. _____ is an information-gathering technique that helps an analyst to find out facts and opinions from a large number of geographically dispersed people.
    A. Questionnaire
    B. Document analysis
    C. JAD session
    D. None of the above

    20._____

21. All of the following are examples of privacy and security risks EXCEPT
    A. viruses
    B. spam
    C. hackers
    D. Trojan horses

    21._____

22. _____ can recover a deleted/damaged file of a computer.
    A. Robotics
    B. Simulation
    C. Both A and B
    D. None of the above

    22._____

23. _____ language is used by the computer to process data.
    A. Binary
    B. Processing
    C. Both A and B
    D. None of the above

    23._____

24. The operating system
    A. enables drawing of a flowchart
    B. provides user-friendly interface
    C. both A and B
    D. none of the above

    24._____

25. _____ is not an application software package.
    A. Microsoft Office
    B. Redhat Linux
    C. Adobe PageMaker
    D. Microsoft PowerPoint

    25._____

# KEY (CORRECT ANSWERS)

| | | | | |
|---|---|---|---|---|
| 1. | A | | 11. | B |
| 2. | D | | 12. | B |
| 3. | A | | 13. | A |
| 4. | A | | 14. | B |
| 5. | A | | 15. | A |
| 6. | A | | 16. | A |
| 7. | A | | 17. | A |
| 8. | C | | 18. | A |
| 9. | B | | 19. | C |
| 10. | D | | 20. | A |

21. B
22. D
23. A
24. B
25. B

# TEST 3

DIRECTIONS: Each question or incomplete statement is followed by several suggested answers or completions. Select the one that BEST answers the question or completes the statement. *PRINT THE LETTER OF THE CORRECT ANSWER IN THE SPACE AT THE RIGHT.*

1. The character repeat rate can be adjusted in   1.____
   A. Control Panel > Keyboard   B. My Computer
   C. Recycle Bin   D. none of the above

2. There are _____ means of using a wireless mouse.   2.____
   A. 1   B. 2
   C. 3   D. none of the above

3. _____ is used for creating and manipulating sound.   3.____
   A. MIDI   B. SIDI
   C. MODO   D. None of the above

4. Picture quality is expressed in   4.____
   A. megapixels   B. hexapixels
   C. both of the above   D. none of the above

5. The microphone port is located on the   5.____
   A. sound card   B. motherboard
   C. driver   D. none of the above

6. The _____ is the peripheral device that transfers the audio from the PC.   6.____
   A. headphones   B. microphone
   C. camera   D. all of the above

7. _____ is a secure connection.   7.____
   A. HTTP   B. TELNET   C. HTTPs   D. RCP

8. A computer can be a client and a server to other computers in a _____ network.   8.____
   A. bus   B. VPN   C. ring   D. peer-to-peer

9. A _____ is used to send a signal at one end of a cable and found at the other end of the cable.   9.____
   A. cable tester   B. toner probe
   C. multimeter   D. none of the above

10. A company's ISP uses _____ to troubleshoot network issues.   10.____
    A. Smart Jack   B. 110 Block   C. 66 Block   D. Demarc

11. A firewall has not blocked a remote web server. To verify this, a _____ can be used.
    A. port scanner
    B. toner probe
    C. both A and B
    D. none of the above

    11.____

12. _____ should be enabled to prevent broadcast storms.
    A. Bonding
    B. Spanning tree
    C. Port mirroring
    D. DHCP

    12.____

13. A _____ network is least likely to collide.
    A. bus
    B. star
    C. ring
    D. mesh

    13.____

14. _____ tests the operation of NIC.
    A. Crossover
    B. Rollover
    C. 568B
    D. Loopback

    14.____

15. Planning includes
    A. conducting preliminary investigation
    B. conducting feasibility study
    C. identifying constraints
    D. all of the above

    15.____

16. Feasibility study types include
    A. technical
    B. economic return
    C. non-economic return
    D. all of the above

    16.____

17. Analysis includes
    A. gathering competent team members
    B. sending instructions to users
    C. documenting the existing system
    D. all of the above

    17.____

18. The design phase includes determining
    A. technical systems configuration
    B. data structure
    C. make or buy decision
    D. all of the above

    18.____

19. Which one of the following is a type of documentation?
    A. System documentation
    B. Document feeder
    C. Audio coding
    D. None of the above

    19.____

20. The implementation phase includes
    A. conducting cutover
    B. training users
    C. managing change
    D. all of the above

    20.____

21. Processing takes place at the
    A. box
    B. CPU
    C. system unit
    D. motherboard

    21.____

22. Memory is of _____ type(s).
    A. one
    B. two
    C. three
    D. four

    22.____

23. The _____ card is used while playing a video game.
    A. sound
    B. graphic
    C. modem
    D. network information

24. To do a specific task, a set of instructions is given to the computer. This most closely describes
    A. software
    B. hardware
    C. Internet browsing
    D. none of the above

25. A user is allowed to analyze and maintain a computer by a program called
    A. Utility
    B. Windows XP
    C. MS Office
    D. Device Driver

## KEY (CORRECT ANSWERS)

1. A
2. B
3. A
4. A
5. A

6. A
7. C
8. D
9. A
10. A

11. A
12. B
13. C
14. D
15. D

16. D
17. C
18. D
19. A
20. D

21. C
22. B
23. A
24. A
25. A

# TEST 4

DIRECTIONS: Each question or incomplete statement is followed by several suggested answers or completions. Select the one that BEST answers the question or completes the statement. *PRINT THE LETTER OF THE CORRECT ANSWER IN THE SPACE AT THE RIGHT.*

1. A(n) _____ is a device resembling a hypodermic needle. 1.____
   A. extractor
   B. detracter
   C. loop back plug
   D. none of the above

2. Which of the following are components of the microcomputer? 2.____
   A. Memory, Unit System
   B. Input device
   C. Output device
   D. All of the above

3. _____ is a common type of keyboard. 3.____
   A. USB
   B. PS/2
   C. Both A and B
   D. None of the above

4. How can we differentiate between a mouse's and keyboard's port? 4.____
   A. Keyboard is purple and mouse is green
   B. Keyboard is green and mouse is purple
   C. Keyboard is blue and mouse is green
   D. None of the above

5. If you reboot your computer and receive an error message of BIOS keyboard, 5.____
   A. the mouse is plugged into the keyboard input
   B. the keyboard is plugged into the mouse input
   C. both A and B
   D. none of the above

6. The mouse settings can be adjusted in 6.____
   A. Control Panel
   B. DOS
   C. My Computer
   D. none of the above

7. _____ prevents the propagating of different departments network broadcasts if they are located on the same switch. 7.____
   A. Hub
   B. VLAN
   C. Firewall
   D. Trunk

8. The most secure protocol for transferring network device configuration is 8.____
   A. TFTP
   B. RCP
   C. SCP
   D. none of the above

9. _____ Internet devices operate the OSI layer. 9.____
   A. One
   B. Two
   C. Three
   D. Four

10. You need to determine which buildings have multimode or single mode fiber. You will use the
    A. security policy
    B. physical network diagram
    C. baseline configuration
    D. none of the above

11. Many users are complaining about network issues. Of the following steps, which will you take FIRST?
    A. Collect information about the symptoms
    B. Make a plan of action and a solution
    C. Document the solution
    D. None of the above

12. Employees utilizing wireless laptops outdoors at the office are experiencing new connectivity problems. _____ is/are most likely causing the problems.
    A. Signal bounce
    B. Antenna distance
    C. Environment factors
    D. None of the above

13. The _____ contain(s) information about unlabeled data center connections.
    A. wiring schematics
    B. emergency call list
    C. procedures manual
    D. none of the above

14. If you have to install a phone that needs only one wire for both data and power to be supplied, _____ must be supported by the switch.
    A. PoE
    B. spanning tree
    C. VLAN
    D. none of the above

15. During the analysis phase, _____ is the type of prototype.
    A. discovery
    B. evolving
    C. functioning
    D. none of the above

16. _____ is a review technique that checks the validity of the documents produced during system analysis.
    A. Structured walkthrough
    B. Prototyping
    C. Joint application
    D. None of the above

17. Implementation classes
    A. describe the user interface
    B. show implementation rules
    C. describe database interactions
    D. none of the above

18. Databases and file definition are prepared in the _____ phase.
    A. implementation
    B. design
    C. analysis
    D. none of the above

19. _____ is requirements analysis deliverables.
    A. Requirement specification
    B. User manual
    C. Design specification
    D. All of the above

20. _____ can help an analyst to work with users to find out system usage.  20._____
    A. Use case              B. Class
    C. Actor                 D. None of the above

21. _____ is a data-transfer technique.  21._____
    A. DMA                   B. CAD
    C. Both A and B          D. None of the above

22. _____ devices are designed under electromechanical principle.  22._____
    A. Input                 B. Output
    C. Storage               D. All of the above

23. A monitor consists of  23._____
    A. BRT                   B. ARU
    C. CRT                   D. none of the above

24. Exception is also known as  24._____
    A. interrupt             B. traps
    C. system calls          D. none of the above

25. _____ is a mutually exclusive operation.  25._____
    A. Signal instruction    B. Wait instruction
    C. Both A and B          D. None of the above

## KEY (CORRECT ANSWERS)

1. A        11. A
2. D        12. C
3. C        13. A
4. A        14. A
5. C        15. A

6. A        16. A
7. B        17. A
8. C        18. A
9. C        19. A
10. B       20. A

21. A
22. A
23. C
24. C
25. C

# EXAMINATION SECTION

## TEST 1

DIRECTIONS: Each question or incomplete statement is followed by several suggested answers or completions. Select the one that BEST answers the question or completes the statement. *PRINT THE LETTER OF THE CORRECT ANSWER IN THE SPACE AT THE RIGHT.*

1. During troubleshooting, you want to see the number of connections which are open on the user machine. The _____ command will be used to see these connections.
    A. Arp
    B. Netstat
    C. NsLookup
    D. Netgear

    1._____

2. Two users want their PCs to be connected for file sharing. A _____ cable would be used to connect their PCs.
    A. crossover
    B. loopback
    C. straight
    D. none of the above

    2._____

3. A remote user complains that he is not able to connect to the office via VPN, though he has established Internet connectivity. What step should you take next to troubleshoot this situation?
    A. Find out if the user is using a valid VPN address and password
    B. Power cycle the VPN concentrator
    C. Reinstall the VPN client
    D. None of the above

    3._____

4. A _____ server limits the availability of types of websites that LAN users have access to.
    A. DHCP
    B. DC
    C. proxy
    D. DNS

    4._____

5. If you are asked by the head of the company to block certain websites for the employees, what should you configure on the workstation to do so?
    A. Port scanner
    B. Antivirus service
    C. Network-based firewall
    D. Host-based firewall

    5._____

6. While troubleshooting a user's problems connecting to their network shares, you find out that the problem lies in the network cabling between the workstation and the switch. If all the other users are able to connect to the network, _____ will probably be the cause.
    A. crosstalk and interference occurring
    B. cable has been damaged or cut within the wall
    C. cable is not punched down properly at the punch panel
    D. none of the above

    6._____

7. Users are reporting that on a Windows network they are not able to access any network resources. The users can ping the IP address and use it to connect to the network resources. The cause of the problem may be
   A. the file server is offline
   B. the DNS server is not resolving properly
   C. the domain controller is not responding
   D. none of the above

7.____

8. If you have to give access to 64 servers on a network, which subnet of the following will provide the required access while conserving the IP address?
   A. 192.168.1.0.23
   B. 192.168.1.0.24
   C. 192.168.1.0.25
   D. 192.168.1.0.26

8.____

9. You are called by a user due to connection issues. You should start troubleshooting by
   A. resetting the router
   B. installing a new NIC
   C. reinstalling the OS
   D. checking the LEDs on NIC

9.____

10. You are called to extend the data circuit to the other side of the office. _____ would be set up at the new location.
    A. ESD
    B. IDF
    C. MDF
    D. EMI

10.____

11. If a connection is punched down and noise is coming across the cable, which of the following tools would be used to identify the problem?
    A. Protocol analyzer
    B. Cable tester
    C. Multimeter
    D. None of the above

11.____

12. You have tested a cable and determined that it can successfully receive and send signals. A _____ can be used to determine the speed and condition of the signal.
    A. TDR
    B. toner probe
    C. voltage event recorder
    D. protocol analyzer

12.____

13. A network has many network printers with server-hosted queues. A client reports that they are not printing. It is verified that all tasks sent from the users' computers to the network printers fail. What should be your next step to troubleshoot this situation?
    A. Replace the printer
    B. Reboot the print server
    C. Power cycle the switch
    D. Try the printer from another PC

13.____

14. A visitor is insisting that he wants to use the company's wireless network on his laptop. DHCP is configured perfectly and a temporary WEP key is assigned to him, but his laptop is still not able to connect to the network because
    A. MAC filtering is enabled of the WAP
    B. the network is out of wireless connections
    C. the DNS server is not working properly
    D. none of the above

14.____

15. An accounting department employee's workstation needs to be connected to the accounting server but is only able to connect to the Internet. The _____ setting should be verified in this case.
    A. VPN  B. WINS  C. DNS  D. VLAN

16. If you discover that the phone company has not installed the smart jack in the right location and it needs to be moved 23 meters to the computer room, a _____ should be requested.
    A. demark extension
    B. 66 block extension
    C. replacement smart jack
    D. none of the above

17. Remote users complain of not being able to access files from the file server. You should first check the
    A. connectivity
    B. access rights
    C. network resources
    D. user accounts

18. You can successfully remote into the company's server but you cannot connect to any other server's directories from the server itself; however, you can ping them via the IP address. What is the problem?
    A. DHCP is not properly configured
    B. DNS is not properly configured
    C. Server is on a different VLAN
    D. None of the above

19. A _____ will be used to relocate a T1 nearer to the switch for connectivity.
    A. patch panel
    B. smart jack
    C. 25 pair cable
    D. none of the above

20. Your organization has 2,500 users, and they have exhausted their Internet bandwidth. You discover that 96% of the traffic is comprised of web browsing. A _____ network device will be added to reduce the amount of Internet bandwidth.
    A. proxy server
    B. load balancer
    C. content switch
    D. none of the above

21. Which document will you reference to discover a rogue WAP?
    A. Policies
    B. Baseline
    C. Wiring schematics
    D. None of the above

22. _____ can allow you to restrict communication between network devices.
    A. ACL  B. CIDR  C. NAT  D. DHCP

23. Your company has a number of traveling sales employees who need secure access to the company's resources from no trusted devices. A _____ VPN solution will be the MOST appropriate for this.
    A. L2TP  B. IPSec  C. PPTP  D. SSL

24. You are troubleshooting a switch and have determined the symptoms. 24._____
What should you do next?
    A. Implement and test solution    B. Find out the scope of the problem
    C. Escalate the issue             D. None of the above

25. In order to find out a physical interface problem, which of the following cables 25._____
would you use?
    A. Loopback     B. Console     C. Rollover     D. Serial

## KEY (CORRECT ANSWERS)

1. B
2. A
3. A
4. C
5. D

6. A
7. B
8. C
9. D
10. B

11. B
12. A
13. D
14. A
15. D

16. A
17. A
18. B
19. B
20. A

21. B
22. A
23. D
24. B
25. A

# TEST 2

DIRECTIONS: Each question or incomplete statement is followed by several suggested answers or completions. Select the one that BEST answers the question or completes the statement. *PRINT THE LETTER OF THE CORRECT ANSWER IN THE SPACE AT THE RIGHT.*

1. You are asked to implement a separate network for the visitors. What would be the MOST cost-effective solution?
    A. Installing a firewall
    B. Creating a VLAN
    C. Installing a VPN
    D. None of the above

2. A user complains that he is not able to send an email to his fellow user at the company and you believe that it is a DNS-related issue. After typing *nslookup*, the _____ command will allow finding out the IP address of the company's mail server.
    A. set type=ptr
    B. set type=mx
    C. set type=soa
    D, none of the above

3. The _____ command will allow you to find out the DNS servers configured on a computer.
    A. nslookup
    B. nbtstat
    C. netstat
    D. none of the above

4. A multiple devices network has to be set with a smaller broadcast domain while remaining on a small budget. The best solution is to
    A. create VLANs
    B. implement more switches
    C. implement more hubs
    D. none of the above

5. If users at your company are not able to connect to servers using the FQDN, the likely cause of this issue would be the _____ is not enabled.
    A. DHCP
    B. DNS
    C. WINS
    D. none of the above

6. If you need to extend the range of the wireless network in your office without running wires throughout the office, which of the following should you implement?
    A. At the end of the office install a repeater
    B. In the middle of the office install a WAP
    C. Both A and B
    D. None of the above

7. You are troubleshooting a network error using a laptop as a network sniffer and are able to see all the communications on the network. What network device is the laptop plugged into?
    A. Router
    B. Gateway
    C. Hub
    D. None of the above

8. To provide the users with better network performance for accessing Internet websites, you should install
   A. traffic shaping
   B. load balancing
   C. caching engine
   D. none of the above

9. After gathering information about a client's network issue and determining the affected area, you will
   A. test the best solution
   B. check for any recent changes in the network
   C. none of the above
   D. both A and B

10. Some users complain that they are not able to access the network. The computers that are not able to access the network carry an IP address of 169.254.0.1. The _____ network service should be checked for troubleshooting.
    A. TFTP
    B. DNS
    C. BOOTP
    D. DHCP

11. You are in charge of several remote servers in the United States. Users call and complain that they are not able to connect to the company's resources that are located on those servers. Which command would you use to verify whether the servers are running?
    A. Ping
    B. Nbstat
    C. Netstat
    D. Telnet

12. A user's star network connected workstation is not able to connect to the network resources. You should first check the
    A. installed network drivers
    B. link lights on the switch
    C. link lights on the network card
    D. none of the above

13. You should be aware of _____ while installing a wireless network in a multiple-floor building.
    A. SSID naming
    B. channel overlap
    C. frequency configuration
    D. none of the above

14. You are contacted by a user. According to him, his system is not able to connect to a file server. After troubleshooting and successfully resolving the issue, you should
    A. create an action plan
    B. document the solution
    C. reboot the server
    D. none of the above

15. A user's computer is affected with an automated application without the user interaction. You should tell the user that this issue is referred to as a
    A. trojan
    B. worm
    C. smurf attack
    D. none of the above

16. You are troubleshooting an application that is frequently terminating. What can be used to determine the problem?
    A. History log
    B. DNS log
    C. Port scanner
    D. Application log

17. A network issue has just been reported to you. Which of the following steps should you take first to troubleshoot the issue?
    A. Ask the user to explain the symptoms in detail
    B. Ask the user about what documentation they had in the past
    C. Record the solution in appropriate logs
    D. None of the above

18. A user complains that after his transfer from the accounting team to HR team he can only print to the accounting team printer and not the HR team printer. What is the cause of this problem?
    A. Wrong DNS
    B. Wrong gateway
    C. Wrong host file
    D. Wrong VLAN

19. If five computers are connected to a single server for file and printing and one computer is not able to connect to the network while the others work properly, this could be caused by
    A. failure of the switch
    B. failure of the server
    C. failure of the NIC
    D. the computer's OS needing to be updated

20. _____ is commonly used to test the fiber connectivity.
    A. Multimeter
    B. Butt set
    C. Toner probe
    D. OTDR

21. A user demands a fault-tolerant server. To provide him with this in a most cost-effective way, you should install
    A. a single router
    B. a single fiber NIC
    C. two NICs for teaming
    D. none of the above

22. A user is having issues accessing the shared resources on the file server. You should first
    A. test the results
    B. identify the symptoms
    C. document the problem
    D. none of the above

23. A user complains that her wireless connection has decreased signal strength, whereas the network configuration has not been changed. The MOST likely cause of the decreased signals is
    A. standards mismatch
    B. incorrect SSID
    C. environmental factors
    D. incorrect encryption

24. A user complains that his wireless 802.11g Internet connection is disrupted. What might be the cause of the problem?
    A. Cell phone
    B. Incandescent light
    C. Cordless phone
    D. Infrared printer

25. You have been asked to retrieve device statistics, errors and information.  25.____
    Which of the following should you use?
    A. SNMP
    B. SMTP
    C. Packet sniffer
    D. TFTP

## KEY (CORRECT ANSWERS)

1. B
2. B
3. A
4. A
5. B

6. B
7. C
8. C
9. B
10. D

11. A
12. C
13. B
14. B
15. B

16. D
17. A
18. D
19. C
20. D

21. C
22. B
23. C
24. C
25. A

# TEST 3

DIRECTIONS: Each question or incomplete statement is followed by several suggested answers or completions. Select the one that BEST answers the question or completes the statement. *PRINT THE LETTER OF THE CORRECT ANSWER IN THE SPACE AT THE RIGHT.*

1. A user is reporting slow network response in his class. The class needs many students to be able to access the same website every day. According to you, which of the following is the BEST remedy for this problem?
   A. Firewall
   B. Caching engine
   C. Fault tolerance
   D. Jitter correction

2. A user complains that he has moved a VoIP phone to a new location. The phone does not start now when it is plugged into the network. The reason for this is that
   A. the phone requires a fiber port
   B. Qos is not enabled on the switch
   C. the switch does not support PoE
   D. none of the above

3. A port scanner is used to
   A. secure switches and routers
   B. find routers with weak passwords
   C. find open ports on network hosts
   D. none of the above

4. A remote web server is not blocked by a firewall. To verify that, a _____ should be used.
   A. port scanner
   B. toner probe
   C. packet injector
   D. none of the above

5. For the purpose of providing redundant paths to network resources, if a link fails, _____ switch features will be needed by you to accomplish the task.
   A. trunking
   B. PoE
   C. VLAN
   D. spanning tree

6. To connect a user to a WPA-encrypted network, you will require a
   A. pre-shared key
   B. PIN
   C. SSID
   D. none of the above

7. Network-based _____ is the most cost-effective technology for protecting a large amount of networked workstations from external attacks.
   A. firewall
   B. IDS
   C. IPS
   D. none of the above

8. After installing and testing a new wireless network for your client and turning wireless access on, you should
   A. document the physical layout
   B. configure wireless adapters
   C. configure the DHCP server
   D. none of the above

9. A ping _____ command would check the loopback adapter of an internal NIC.
   A. 127.1.1.1
   B. 127.0.0.1
   C. 127.127.0.0
   D. none of the above

10. To prevent broadcast storms for your client, you should enable
    A. DHCP
    B. port mirroring
    C. bonding
    D. spanning tree

11. You are configuring a router for SOHO network. You have disabled DHCP service and replaced the IP address scheme on the router. Now you have to establish the connection while keeping the router's current configuration state. What would be the BEST solution?
    A. Assign a static IP address so the PC matches the router
    B. Use APIPA to connect the PC to the router
    C. Both A and B
    D. None of the above

12. When you are configuring a wireless access point, select the channel
    A. frequency range least used in a given area
    B. closest to that configured on neighboring access points
    C. that is the same channel configured on the neighboring access points
    D. none of the above

13. A client has accidentally unplugged the network cable of their computer (in a wired bus topology environment). Which of the following is TRUE?
    A. It will not function until the wires are reconnected
    B. It will function with minimal downtime
    C. It will function with no downtime
    D. None of the above

14. A user complains that he can access the network shares and his email but cannot access any website. Which command tools will you use to begin troubleshooting?
    A. Trace route to any website to determine where the disconnection is happening
    B. Use route add command
    C. Use ping command
    D. None of the above

15. Users at a branch office complain that access to static web content is very slow from their location. Which of the following will improve WAN utilization?
    A. A traffic shaper
    B. An application level firewall
    C. A caching proxy server at the branch
    D. None of the above

16. Your head asks you to verify the available phone numbers at your company. Which of the following should you use to verify the available numbers?
    A. Multimeter
    B. Toner probe
    C. Punch down tool
    D. Butt set

17. You need to run a network for your company, which should be able to handle 30 Mbps data-transfer speeds while keeping the installation cost of the network down. Which cable types would you prefer?
    A. CAT3
    B. CAT6
    C. CAT5e
    D. CAT1

18. You are troubleshooting an issue where a computer is not connecting to the Internet employing a wireless access point. The computer is transferring files locally to the other machines but is unable to reach the Internet. The IP address and default gateways are both on the 182.158.1.0/24. The problem is that the computer
    A. gateway is not routing to a public IP address
    B. is using an invalid IP address
    C. is not using a private IP address
    D. none of the above

19. You have to set up a connection that enables visitors to connect to the Internet but not the server, while employees will be able to connect to both. The same switch manages all of the connections. What should be used to meet these requirements?
    A. OSPF
    B. RIP
    C. Post trunking
    D. VLAN

20. An employee kitchen area is added to your office. No changes have been made in the work area and equipment, but the employees are having a wireless connectivity problem. What is the cause of the problem?
    A. Interference
    B. Distance
    C. Encryption
    D. None of the above

21. If the staff is trained about implementing a set of procedures and policies that makes clear that corporation information is confidential, _____ can be prevented.
    A. social engineering
    B. patch management
    C. smurf attacks
    D. none of the above

22. A user support analyst must be able to manage
    A. his time
    B. his client's time
    C. both A and B
    D. managing time is not necessary in this matter

23. A user support analyst must be able to
    A. consider the relative costs
    B. consider the benefits of potential actions to select the most appropriate one
    C. both A and B
    D. none of the above

24. A user support analyst should
    A. always solve the problems himself
    B. teach users to solve the minor problems themselves
    C. never let users solve the problem
    D. none of the above

25. The user support analyst should have the ability to
    A. communicate information and ideas
    B. read and understand information
    C. identify and understand the speech of another person
    D. all of the above

## KEY (CORRECT ANSWERS)

| | | | | |
|---|---|---|---|---|
| 1. | B | | 11. | A |
| 2. | C | | 12. | A |
| 3. | C | | 13. | A |
| 4. | A | | 14. | A |
| 5. | D | | 15. | C |
| 6. | A | | 16. | D |
| 7. | A | | 17. | C |
| 8. | A | | 18. | A |
| 9. | B | | 19. | D |
| 10. | D | | 20. | A |

| | |
|---|---|
| 21. | A |
| 22. | C |
| 23. | C |
| 24. | B |
| 25. | D |

# TEST 4

DIRECTIONS: Each question or incomplete statement is followed by several suggested answers or completions. Select the one that BEST answers the question or completes the statement. *PRINT THE LETTER OF THE CORRECT ANSWER IN THE SPACE AT THE RIGHT.*

1. You are troubleshooting the phone service at a site and discover that there is no dial tone present in the connection on block 65. Which tool would you use to check the connection at the demarcation point?  
   A. Toner probe    B. Multimeter    C. Cable tester    D. Butt set     1.____

2. A client calls you to troubleshoot his machine and you need to open connections and see the current NetBIOS configuration. Which command would you use to display this information?  
   A. nbstat    B. msconfig    C. netstat    D. ipconfig     2.____

3. A client asks you to implement a new wireless network and run the highest level of wireless encryption. You should run  
   A. WEP    B. WPA2 TKIP    C. WPAS AES    D. TTL     3.____

4. Which of the following tools is used for capturing username and passwords on a network?  
   A. Proxy server    B. Sniffer    C. Firewall    D. Honey pot     4.____

5. A company consists of one headquarters and eight remote sites. The remote sites just need to communicate with the headquarters. Which topology is BEST for the company?  
   A. Mesh    B. Star    C. Hybrid    D. Ring     5.____

6. Which of the following command line tools would you use to verify DNS functionality?  
   A. netstat    B. arp    C. dig    D. traceroute     6.____

7. Which of the following would you use to provide the highest level of security to a newly installed wireless router?  
   A. SSL    B. WEP    C. WPA    D. IPSec     7.____

8. An application layer firewall can filter _____, while a network layer firewall cannot.     8.____
   A. HTTP URLs    B. ICMP  
   C. Telnet traffic    D. HTTP traffic

9. What should be used for the purpose of connecting multiple network hosts when the physical signal is being repeated to all ports?     9.____
   A. Bridge    B. Hub    C. Router    D. Switch

161

10. While troubleshooting you need to catch a specific NICs MAC address. While you know the IP address of the NIC, _____ would enable you to discover the MAC address without going to that specific computer physically.
    A. netstat   B. ping   C. nbstat   D. arp

11. A VoIP telephone with a built-in hub is plugged into a single network, using both of the ports (hub port and telephone port). Suddenly, the network starts to experience lag because of the increase in traffic. What would help to avoid this situation in the future?
    A. VLANs
    B. Trunking
    C. Port mirroring
    D. Spanning tree

12. _____ is the MOST secure access method.
    A. RSH   B. SNMPv1   C. SFTP   D. RCP

13. If you need to access files on a remote server, _____ would be used.
    A. ARP   B. FTP   C. SIP   D. NTP

14. _____ is 568B standard.
    A. Logical network diagram
    B. Network baseline
    C. Wiring schematic
    D. None of the above

15. A user complains that on a wireless network he can connect to local resources but cannot connect to the Internet. Which of the following might be the reason?
    A. The gateway is not configured on the router
    B. The wireless network card is not in range
    C. The wireless network card is not working
    D. None of the above

16. _____ is a client-server based authentication software system that keeps user profiles in a central database.
    A. RADIUS   B. MSCHAp   C. EAP   D. CHAP

17. _____ is an authentication protocol the employs plain text for transmitting passwords over the internet.
    A. Kerberos   B. CHAP   C. PAP   D. RADIUS

18. A user wants to bond his new printer with his PDA. What is the BEST technology to describe the type of wireless printer?
    A. Wi-Fi   B. Bluetooth   C. IEEE 1394   D. 802.11a

19. Many workstations have lost network connectivity in network. Which of the following steps should you take to troubleshoot the issue?
    A. Document all possible causes
    B. Reboot the computer
    C. Escalate the issue to a senior network associate
    D. None of the above

3 (#4)

20. You need to provide a solution that will allow 500 users of a remote site to access the Internet using only one public routable IP address, allowing direct user access to the Internet. What is the BEST technology to implement?
    A. DNS  B. PAT  C. VPN  D. DHCP

    20.____

21. You discover that unencrypted passwords are being sent over the network. Which network monitoring utility was used to find this out?
    A. Network scanner  B. Packet sniffer
    C. Throughput tester  D. None of the above

    21.____

22. _____ would need to be installed to connect a fiber NIC with an Ethernet backbone.
    A. Bridge  B. Hub
    C. Repeater  D. None of the above

    22.____

23. _____ is the MOST essential component for providing user support.
    A. Communication  B. Knowledge
    C. Experience  D. None of the above

    23.____

24. To get to the heart of the problem, the support analyst must
    A. listen to the user  B. not ask questions to the user
    C. ask the right question  D. both A and C

    24.____

25. The user should be kept _____ by the support analyst.
    A. informed of progress  B. informed of expected next steps
    C. both A and B  D. informed of all technical details

    25.____

## KEY (CORRECT ANSWERS)

1. D
2. A
3. C
4. B
5. D

6. C
7. C
8. A
9. B
10. D

11. D
12. C
13. B
14. C
15. A

16. A
17. C
18. B
19. C
20. C

21. B
22. B
23. A
24. D
25. C

# GLOSSARY OF COMPUTER TERMS

## Contents

**Basic**                                                       Page

application & app----disk                                       1
drive----function keys                                          2
graphics----modem                                               3
monitor----PDA                                                  4
platform----www                                                 5

**Reference**

65xx----Amiga                                                   6
AmigaOS----ASCII                                                7
ASK----BeOS                                                     8
beta byte                                                       9
bytecode ----character set                                      10
CISC---- Cray                                                   11
crippleware---- DRM                                             12
DTML----FAQ                                                     13
Fire Wire----FTP                                                14
Gateway----HP-UX                                                15
HTML----interactive fiction                                     16
interpreted----JavaScript                                       17.
jiffy----Llinux                                                 18
Lisp----Mac OS X                                                19
machine language----MIME                                        20
MMX----NetBSD                                                   21
netiquette----object-oriented                                   22
ObjectiveC & ObjC ---- partition                                23
Pascal----Power PC                                              24
proprietary----RISC                                             25
robot----server                                                 26
SGML----Sugar                                                   27
SunOS----UNIX                                                   28
upload----VAX                                                   29
vector----VRML                                                  30
W3C----Windows 3.1                                              31
Windows CE----WYSIWYM                                           32
X-Face----XUL                                                   33
Y2K----Z-Machine                                                34
Z80----Zoomer                                                   35

# GLOSSARY OF COMPUTER TERMS

## Basic

**application & app**
An application (often called "app" for short) is simply a program with a GUI. Note that it is different from an applet.

**boot**
Starting up an OS is booting it. If the computer is already running, it is more often called rebooting.

**browser**
A browser is a program used to browse the web. Some common browsers include Netscape, MSIE (Microsoft Internet Explorer), Safari, Lynx, Mosaic, Amaya, Arena, Chimera, Opera, Cyberdog, HotJava, etc.

**bug**
A bug is a mistake in the design of something, especially software. A really severe bug can cause something to crash.

**chat**
Chatting is like e-mail, only it is done instantaneously and can directly involve multiple people at once. While e-mail now relies on one more or less standard protocol, chatting still has a couple competing ones. Of particular note are IRC and Instant Messenger. One step beyond chatting is called MUDding.

**click**
To press a mouse button. When done twice in rapid succession, it is referred to as a double-click.

**cursor**
A point of attention on the computer screen, often marked with a flashing line or block. Text typed into the computer will usually appear at the cursor.

**database**
A database is a collection of data, typically organized to make common retrievals easy and efficient. Some common database programs include Oracle, Sybase, Postgres, Informix, Filemaker, Adabas, etc.

**desktop**
A desktop system is a computer designed to sit in one position on a desk somewhere and not move around. Most general purpose computers are desktop systems. Calling a system a desktop implies nothing about its platform. The fastest desktop system at any given time is typically either an Alpha or PowerPC based system, but the SPARC and PA-RISC based systems are also often in the running. Industrial strength desktops are typically called workstations.

**directory**
Also called "folder", a directory is a collection of files typically created for organizational purposes. Note that a directory is itself a file, so a directory can generally contain other directories. It differs in this way from a partition.

**disk**
A disk is a physical object used for storing data. It will not forget its data when it loses power. It is always used in conjunction with a disk drive. Some disks can be removed from their drives, some cannot. Generally it is possible to write new information to a disk in addition to reading data from it, but this is not always the case.

**drive**
A device for storing and/or retrieving data. Some drives (such as disk drives, zip drives, and tape drives) are typically capable of having new data written to them, but some others (like CD-ROMs or DVD-ROMs) are not. Some drives have random access (like disk drives, zip drives, CD-ROMs, and DVD-ROMs), while others only have sequential access (like tape drives).

**e-book**
The concept behind an e-book is that it should provide all the functionality of an ordinary book but in a manner that is (overall) less expensive and more environmentally friendly. The actual term e-book is somewhat confusingly used to refer to a variety of things: custom software to play e-book titles, dedicated hardware to play e-book titles, and the e-book titles themselves. Individual e-book titles can be free or commercial (but will always be less expensive than their printed counterparts) and have to be loaded into a player to be read. Players vary wildly in capability level. Basic ones allow simple reading and bookmarking; better ones include various features like hypertext, illustrations, audio, and even limited video. Other optional features allow the user to mark-up sections of text, leave notes, circle or diagram things, highlight passages, program or customize settings, and even use interactive fiction. There are many types of e-book; a couple popular ones include the Newton book and Palm DOC.

**e-mail**
E-mail is short for electronic mail. It allows for the transfer of information from one computer to another, provided that they are hooked up via some sort of network (often the Internet. E-mail works similarly to FAXing, but its contents typically get printed out on the other end only on demand, not immediately and automatically as with FAX. A machine receiving e-mail will also not reject other incoming mail messages as a busy FAX machine will; rather they will instead be queued up to be received after the current batch has been completed. E-mail is only seven-bit clean, meaning that you should not expect anything other than ASCII data to go through uncorrupted without prior conversion via something like uucode or bcode. Some mailers will do some conversion automatically, but unless you know your mailer is one of them, you may want to do the encoding manually.

**file**
A file is a unit of (usually named) information stored on a computer.

**firmware**
Sort of in-between hardware and software, firmware consists of modifiable programs embedded in hardware. Firmware updates should be treated with care since they can literally destroy the underlying hardare if done improperly. There are also cases where neglecting to apply a firmware update can destroy the underlying hardware, so user beware.

**floppy**
An extremely common type of removable disk. Floppies do not hold too much data, but most computers are capable of reading them. Note though that there are different competing format used for floppies, so that a floppy written by one type of computer might not directly work on another. Also sometimes called "diskette".

**format**
The manner in which data is stored; its organization. For example, VHS, SVHS, and Beta are three different formats of video tape. They are not 100% compatible with each other, but information can be transferred from one to the other with the proper equipment (but not always without loss; SVHS contains more information than either of the other two). Computer information can be stored in literally hundreds of different formats, and can represent text, sounds, graphics, animations, etc. Computer information can be exchanged via different computer types provided both computers can interpret the format used.

**function keys**
On a computer keyboard, the keys that start with an "F" that are usually (but not always) found on the top row. They are meant to perform user-defined tasks.

**graphics**
Anything visually displayed on a computer that is not text.
**hardware**
The physical portion of the computer.
**hypertext**
A hypertext document is like a text document with the ability to contain pointers to other regions of (possibly other) hypertext documents.
**Internet**
The Internet is the world-wide network of computers. There is only one Internet, and thus it is typically capitalized (although it is sometimes referred to as "the 'net"). It is different from an intranet.
**keyboard**
A keyboard on a computer is almost identical to a keyboard on a typewriter. Computer keyboards will typically have extra keys, however. Some of these keys (common examples include Control, Alt, and Meta) are meant to be used in conjunction with other keys just like shift on a regular typewriter. Other keys (common examples include Insert, Delete, Home, End, Help, function keys,etc.) are meant to be used independently and often perform editing tasks. Keyboards on different platforms will often look slightly different and have somewhat different collections of keys. Some keyboards even have independent shift lock and caps lock keys. Smaller keyboards with only math-related keys are typically called "keypads".
**language**
Computer programs can be written in a variety of different languages. Different languages are optimized for different tasks. Common languages include Java, C, C++, ForTran, Pascal, Lisp, and BASIC. Some people classify languages into two categories, higher-level and lower-level. These people would consider assembly language and machine language lower-level languages and all other languages higher-level. In general, higher-level languages can be either interpreted or compiled; many languages allow both, but some are restricted to one or the other. Many people do not consider machine language and assembly language at all when talking about programming languages.
**laptop**
A laptop is any computer designed to do pretty much anything a desktop system can do but run for a short time (usually two to five hours) on batteries. They are designed to be carried around but are not particularly convenient to carry around. They are significantly more expensive than desktop systems and have far worse battery life than PDAs. Calling a system a laptop implies nothing about its platform. By far the fastest laptops are the PowerPC based Macintoshes.
**memory**
Computer memory is used to temporarily store data. In reality, computer memory is only capable of remembering sequences of zeros and ones, but by utilizing the binary number system it is possible to produce arbitrary rational numbers and through clever formatting all manner of representations of pictures, sounds, and animations. The most common types of memory are RAM, ROM, and flash.
**MHz & megahertz**
One megahertz is equivalent to 1000 kilohertz, or 1,000,000 hertz. The clock speed of the main processor of many computers is measured in MHz, and is sometimes (quite misleadingly) used to represent the overall speed of a computer. In fact, a computer's speed is based upon many factors, and since MHz only reveals how many clock cycles the main processor has per second (saying nothing about how much is actually accomplished per cycle), it can really only accurately be used to gauge two computers with the same generation and family of processor plus similar configurations of memory, co-processors, and other peripheral hardware.
**modem**
A modem allows two computers to communicate over ordinary phone lines. It derives its name

from **mod**ulate / **dem**odulate, the process by which it converts digital computer data back and forth for use with an analog phone line.
## monitor
The screen for viewing computer information is called a monitor.
## mouse
In computer parlance a mouse can be both the physical object moved around to control a pointer on the screen, and the pointer itself. Unlike the animal, the proper plural of computer mouse is "mouses".
## multimedia
This originally indicated a capability to work with and integrate various types of things including audio, still graphics, and especially video. Now it is more of a marketing term and has little real meaning. Historically the Amiga was the first multimedia machine. Today in addition to AmigaOS, IRIX and Solaris are popular choices for high-end multimedia work.
## NC
The term **n**etwork **c**omputer refers to any (usually desktop) computer system that is designed to work as part of a network rather than as a stand-alone machine. This saves money on hardware, software, and maintenance by taking advantage of facilities already available on the network. The term "Internet appliance" is often used interchangeably with NC.
## network
A network (as applied to computers) typically means a group of computers working together. It can also refer to the physical wire etc. connecting the computers.
## notebook
A notebook is a small laptop with similar price, performance, and battery life.
## organizer
An organizer is a tiny computer used primarily to store names, addresses, phone numbers, and date book information. They usually have some ability to exchange information with desktop systems. They boast even better battery life than PDAs but are far less capable. They are extremely inexpensive but are typically incapable of running any special purpose applications and are thus of limited use.
## OS
The **o**perating **s**ystem is the program that manages a computer's resources. Common OSes include Windows '95, MacOS, Linux, Solaris, AmigaOS, AIX, Windows NT, etc.
## PC
The term **p**ersonal **c**omputer properly refers to any desktop, laptop, or notebook computer system. Its use is inconsistent, though, and some use it to specifically refer to x86 based systems running MS-DOS, MS-Windows, GEOS, or OS/2. This latter use is similar to what is meant by a WinTel system.
## PDA
A **p**ersonal **d**igital **a**ssistant is a small battery-powered computer intended to be carried around by the user rather than left on a desk. This means that the processor used ought to be power-efficient as well as fast, and the OS ought to be optimized for hand-held use. PDAs typically have an instant-on feature (they would be useless without it) and most are grayscale rather than color because of battery life issues. Most have a pen interface and come with a detachable stylus. None use mouses. All have some ability to exchange data with desktop systems. In terms of raw capabilities, a PDA is more capable than an organizer and less capable than a laptop (although some high-end PDAs beat out some low-end laptops). By far the most popular PDA is the Pilot, but other common types include Newtons, Psions, Zauri, Zoomers, and Windows CE hand-helds. By far the fastest current PDA is the Newton (based around a StrongARM RISC processor). Other PDAs are optimized for other tasks; few computers are as personal as PDAs and care must be taken in their purchase. Feneric's PDA / Handheld Comparison Page is perhaps the most detailed comparison of PDAs and handheld computers

to be found anywhere on the web.

**platform**
Roughly speaking, a platform represents a computer's family. It is defined by both the processor type on the hardware side and the OS type on the software side. Computers belonging to different platforms cannot typically run each other's programs (unless the programs are written in a language like Java).

**portable**
If something is portable it can be easily moved from one type of computer to another. The verb "to port" indicates the moving itself.

**printer**
A printer is a piece of hardware that will print computer information onto paper.

**processor**
The processor (also called central processing unit, or CPU) is the part of the computer that actually works with the data and runs the programs. There are two main processor types in common usage today: CISC and RISC. Some computers have more than one processor and are thus called "multiprocessor". This is distinct from multitasking. Advertisers often use megahertz numbers as a means of showing a processor's speed. This is often extremely misleading; megahertz numbers are more or less meaningless when compared across different types of processors.

**program**
A program is a series of instructions for a computer, telling it what to do or how to behave. The terms "application" and "app" mean almost the same thing (albeit applications generally have GUIs). It is however different from an applet. Program is also the verb that means to create a program, and a programmer is one who programs.

**run**
Running a program is how it is made to do something. The term "execute" means the same thing.

**software**
The non-physical portion of the computer; the part that exists only as data; the programs. Another term meaning much the same is "code".

**spreadsheet**
An program used to perform various calculations. It is especially popular for financial applications. Some common spreadsheets include Lotus 123, Excel, OpenOffice Spreadsheet, Octave, Gnumeric, AppleWorks Spreadsheet, Oleo, and GeoCalc.

**user**
The operator of a computer.

**word processor**
A program designed to help with the production of textual documents, like letters and memos. Heavier duty work can be done with a desktop publisher. Some common word processors include MS-Word, OpenOffice Write, WordPerfect, AbiWord, AppleWorks Write, and GeoWrite.

**www**
The World-Wide-Web refers more or less to all the publically accessible documents on the Internet. It is used quite loosely, and sometimes indicates only HTML files and sometimes FTP and Gopher files, too. It is also sometimes just referred to as "the web".

# 6

## Reference

### 65xx
The 65xx series of processors includes the 6502, 65C02, 6510, 8502, 65C816, 65C816S, etc. It is a CISC design and is not being used in too many new stand-alone computer systems, but is still being used in embedded systems, game systems (such as the Super NES), and processor enhancement add-ons for older systems. It was originally designed by MOS Technologies, but is now produced by The Western Design Center, Inc. It was the primary processor for many extremely popular systems no longer being produced, including the Commodore 64, the Commodore 128, and all the Apple ][ series machines.

### 68xx
The 68xx series of processors includes the 6800, 6805, 6809, 68000, 68020, 68030, 68040, 68060, etc. It is a CISC design and is not being used in too many new stand-alone computer systems, but is still being used heavily in embedded systems. It was originally designed by Motorola and was the primary processor for older generations of many current machines, including Macintoshes, Amigas, Sun workstations, HP workstations, etc. and the primary processor for many systems no longer being produced, such as the TRS-80. The PowerPC was designed in part to be its replacement.

### a11y
Commonly used to abbreviate the word "accessibility". There are eleven letters between the "a" and the "y".

### ADA
An object-oriented language at one point popular for military and some academic software. Lately C++ and Java have been getting more attention.

### AI
Artificial intelligence is the concept of making computers do tasks once considered to require thinking. AI makes computers play chess, recognize handwriting and speech, helps suggest prescriptions to doctors for patients based on imput symptoms, and many other tasks, both mundane and not.

### AIX
The industrial strength OS designed by IBM to run on PowerPC and x86 based machines. It is a variant of UNIX and is meant to provide more power than OS/2.

### AJaX
AJaX is a little like DHTML, but it adds asynchronous communication between the browser and Web site via either XML or JSON to achieve performance that often rivals desktop applications.

### Alpha
An Alpha is a RISC processor invented by Digital and currently produced by Digital/Compaq and Samsung. A few different OSes run on Alpha based machines including Digital UNIX, Windows NT, Linux, NetBSD, and AmigaOS. Historically, at any given time, the fastest processor in the world has usually been either an Alpha or a PowerPC (with sometimes SPARCs and PA-RISCs making the list), but Compaq has recently announced that there will be no further development of this superb processor instead banking on the release of the somewhat suspect Merced.

### AltiVec
AltiVec (also called the "Velocity Engine") is a special extension built into some PowerPC CPUs to provide better performance for certain operations, most notably graphics and sound. It is similar to MMX on the x86 CPUs. Like MMX, it requires special software for full performance benefits to be realized.

### Amiga

A platform originally created and only produced by Commodore, but now owned by Gateway 2000 and produced by it and a few smaller companies. It was historically the first multimedia machine and gave the world of computing many innovations. It is now primarily used for audio / video applications; in fact, a decent Amiga system is less expensive than a less capable video editing system. Many music videos were created on Amigas, and a few television series and movies had their special effects generated on Amigas. Also, Amigas can be readily synchronized with video cameras, so typically when a computer screen appears on television or in a movie and it is not flickering wildly, it is probably an Amiga in disguise. Furthermore, many coin-operated arcade games are really Amigas packaged in stand-up boxes. Amigas have AmigaOS for their OS. New Amigas have either a PowerPC or an Alpha for their main processor and a 68xx processor dedicated to graphics manipulation. Older (and low end) Amigas do everything with just a 68xx processor.

**AmigaOS**
The OS used by Amigas. AmigaOS combines the functionality of an OS and a window manager and is fully multitasking. AmigaOS boasts a pretty good selection of games (many arcade games are in fact written on Amigas) but has limited driver support. AmigaOS will run on 68xx, Alpha, and PowerPC based machines.

**Apple ][**
The Apple ][ computer sold millions of units and is generally considered to have been the first home computer with a 1977 release date. It is based on the 65xx family of processors. The earlier Apple I was only available as a build-it-yourself kit.

**AppleScript**
A scripting language for Mac OS computers.

**applet**
An applet differs from an application in that is not meant to be run stand-alone but rather with the assistance of another program, usually a browser.

**AppleTalk**
AppleTalk is a protocol for computer networks. It is arguably inferior to TCP/IP.

**Aqua**
The default window manager for Mac OS X.

**Archie**
Archie is a system for searching through FTP archives for particular files. It tends not to be used too much anymore as more general modern search engines are significantly more capable.

**ARM**
An ARM is a RISC processor invented by Advanced RISC Machines, currently owned by Intel, and currently produced by both the above and Digital/Compaq. ARMs are different from most other processors in that they were not designed to maximize speed but rather to maximize speed per power consumed. Thus ARMs find most of their use on hand-held machines and PDAs. A few different OSes run on ARM based machines including Newton OS, JavaOS, and (soon) Windows CE and Linux. The StrongARM is a more recent design of the original ARM, and it is both faster and more power efficient than the original.

**ASCII**
The ASCII character set is the most popular one in common use. People will often refer to a bare text file without complicated embedded format instructions as an ASCII file, and such files can usually be transferred from one computer system to another with relative ease. Unfortunately there are a few minor variations of it that pop up here and there, and if you receive a text file that seems subtly messed up with punctuation marks altered or upper and lower case reversed, you are probably encountering one of the ASCII variants. It is usually fairly straightforward to translate from one ASCII variant to another, though. The ASCII character set is seven bit while pure binary is usually eight bit, so transferring a binary file through ASCII channels will result in corruption and loss of data. Note also that the ASCII character set is a

subset of the Unicode character set.
## ASK
A protocol for an infrared communications port on a device. It predates the IrDA compliant infrared communications protocol and is not compatible with it. Many devices with infrared communications support both, but some only support one or the other.
## assembly language
Assembly language is essentially machine language that has had some of the numbers replaced by somewhat easier to remember mnemonics in an attempt to make it more human-readable. The program that converts assembly language to machine language is called an assembler. While assembly language predates FORTRAN, it is not typically what people think of when they discuss computer languages.
## Atom
Atom is an intended replacement for RSS and like it is used for syndicating a web site's content. It is currently not nearly as popular or well-supported by software applications, however.
## authoring system
Any GUIs method of designing new software can be called an authoring system. Any computer language name with the word "visual" in front of it is probably a version of that language built with some authoring system capabilities. It appears that the first serious effort to produce a commercial quality authoring system took place in the mid eighties for the Amiga.
## AWK
AWK is an interpreted language developed in 1977 by Aho, Weinberger, & Kernighan. It gets its name from its creators' initials. It is not particularly fast, but it was designed for creating small throwaway programs rather than full-blown applications -- it is designed to make the writing of the program fast, not the program itself. It is quite portable with versions existing for numerous platforms, including a free GNU version. Plus, virtually every version of UNIX in the world comes with AWK built-in.
## BASIC
The **B**eginners' **A**ll-purpose **S**ymbolic **I**nstruction **C**ode is a computer language developed by Kemeny & Kurtz in 1964. Although it is traditionally interpreted, compilers exist for many platforms. While the interpreted form is typically fairly slow, the compiled form is often quite fast, usually faster than Pascal. The biggest problem with BASIC is portability; versions for different machines are often completely unlike each other; Amiga BASIC at first glance looks more like Pascal, for example. Portability problems actually go beyond even the cross platform level; in fact, most machines have multiple versions of incompatible BASICs available for use. The most popular version of BASIC today is called Visual BASIC. Like all BASICs it has portability issues, but it has some of the advantages of an authoring system so it is relatively easy to use.
## baud
A measure of communications speed, used typically for modems indicating how many bits per second can be transmitted.
## BBS
A **b**ulletin **b**oard **s**ystem is a computer that can be directly connected to via modem and provides various services like e-mail, chatting, newsgroups, and file downloading. BBSs have waned in popularity as more and more people are instead connecting to the Internet, but they are still used for product support and local area access. Most current BBSs provide some sort of gateway connection to the Internet.
## bcode
Identical in intent to uucode, bcode is slightly more efficient and more portable across different computer types. It is the preferred method used by MIME.
## BeOS
A lightweight OS available for both PowerPC and x86 based machines. It is often referred to simply as "Be".

**beta**
A beta version of something is not yet ready for prime time but still possibly useful to related developers and other interested parties. Expect beta software to crash more than properly released software does. Traditionally beta versions (of commercial software) are distributed only to selected testers who are often then given a discount on the proper version after its release in exchange for their testing work. Beta versions of non-commercial software are more often freely available to anyone who has an interest.

**binary**
There are two meanings for binary in common computer usage. The first is the name of the number system in which there are only zeros and ones. This is important to computers because all computer data is ultimately a series of zeros and ones, and thus can be represented by binary numbers. The second is an offshoot of the first; data that is not meant to be intepreted through a common character set (like ASCII) is typically referred to as binary data. Pure binary data is typically eight bit data, and transferring a binary file through ASCII channels without prior modification will result in corruption and loss of data. Binary data can be turned into ASCII data via uucoding or bcoding.

**bit**
A bit can either be on or off; one or zero. All computer data can ultimately be reduced to a series of bits. The term is also used as a (very rough) measure of sound quality, color quality, and even procesor capability by considering the fact that series of bits can represent binary numbers. For example (without getting too technical), an eight bit image can contain at most 256 distinct colors while a sixteen bit image can contain at most 65,536 distinct colors.

**bitmap**
A bitmap is a simplistic representation of an image on a computer, simply indicating whether or not pixels are on or off, and sometimes indicating their color. Often fonts are represented as bitmaps. The term "pixmap" is sometimes used similarly; typically when a distinction is made, pixmap refers to color images and bitmap refers to monochrome images.

**blog**
Short for web log, a blog (or weblog, or less commonly, 'blog) is a web site containing periodic (usually frequent) posts. Blogs are usually syndicated via either some type of RSS or Atom and often supports TrackBacks. It is not uncommon for blogs to function much like newspaper columns. A blogger is someone who writes for and maintains a blog.

**boolean**
Boolean algebra is the mathematics of base two numbers. Since base two numbers have only two values, zero and one, there is a good analogy between base two numbers and the logical values "true" & "false". In common usage, booleans are therefore considered to be simple logical values like true & false and the operations that relate them, most typically "and", "or" and "not". Since everyone has a basic understanding of the concepts of true & false and basic conjunctions, everyone also has a basic understanding of boolean concepts -- they just may not realize it.

**byte**
A byte is a grouping of bits. It is typically eight bits, but there are those who use non-standard byte sizes. Bytes are usually measured in large groups, and the term "kilobyte" (often abbreviated as K) means one-thousand twenty-four (1024) bytes; the term "megabyte" (often abbreviated as M) means one-thousand twenty-four (1024) K; the term gigabyte (often abbreviated as G) means one-thousand twenty-four (1024) M; and the term "terabyte" (often abbreviated as T) means one-thousand twenty-four (1024) G. Memory is typically measured in kilobytes or megabytes, and disk space is typically measured in megabytes or gigabytes. Note that the multipliers here are 1024 instead of the more common 1000 as would be used in the metric system. This is to make it easier to work with the binary number system. Note also that some hardware manufacturers will use the smaller 1000 multiplier on M & G quantities to make

their disk drives seem larger than they really are; buyer beware.

**bytecode**

Sometimes computer languages that are said to be either interpreted or compiled are in fact neither and are more accurately said to be somewhere in between. Such languages are compiled into bytecode which is then interpreted on the target system. Bytecode tends to be binary but will work on any machine with the appropriate runtime environment (or virtual machine) for it.

**C**

C is one of the most popular computer languages in the world, and quite possibly *the* most popular. It is a compiled langauge widely supported on many platforms. It tends to be more portable than FORTRAN but less portable than Java; it has been standardized by ANSI as "ANSI C" -- older versions are called either "K&R C" or "Kernighan and Ritchie C" (in honor of C's creators), or sometimes just "classic C". Fast and simple, it can be applied to all manner of general purpose tasks. C compilers are made by several companies, but the free GNU version (gcc) is still considered one of the best. Newer C-like object-oriented languages include both Java and C++.

**C#**

C# is a compiled object-oriented language based heavily on C++ with some Java features.

**C++**

C++ is a compiled object-oriented language. Based heavily on C, C++ is nearly as fast and can often be thought of as being just C with added features. It is currently probably the second most popular object-oriented language, but it has the drawback of being fairly complex -- the much simpler but somewhat slower Java is probably the most popular object-oriented language. Note that C++ was developed independently of the somewhat similar Objective-C; it is however related to Objective-C++.

**C64/128**

The Commodore 64 computer to this day holds the record for being the most successful model of computer ever made with even the lowest estimates being in the tens of millions. Its big brother, the Commodore 128, was not quite as popular but still sold several million units. Both units sported ROM-based BASIC and used it as a default "OS". The C128 also came with CP/M (it was a not-often-exercized option on the C64). In their later days they were also packaged with GEOS. Both are based on 65xx family processors. They are still in use today and boast a friendly and surprisingly active user community. There is even a current effort to port Linux to the C64 and C128 machines.

**CDE**

The **c**ommon **d**esktop **e**nvironment is a popular commercial window manager (and much more -- as its name touts, it is more of a desktop environment) that runs under X-Windows. Free work-alike versions are also available.

**chain**

Some computer devices support chaining, the ability to string multiple devices in a sequence plugged into just one computer port. Often, but not always, such a chain will require some sort of terminator to mark the end. For an example, a SCSI scanner may be plugged into a SCSI CD-ROM drive that is plugged into a SCSI hard drive that is in turn plugged into the main computer. For all these components to work properly, the scanner would also have to have a proper terminator in use. Device chaining has been around a long time, and it is interesting to note that C64/128 serial devices supported it from the very beginning. Today the most common low-cost chainable devices in use support USB while the fastest low-cost chainable devices in use support FireWire.

**character set**

Since in reality all a computer can store are series of zeros and ones, representing common things like text takes a little work. The solution is to view the series of zeros and ones instead as a sequence of bytes, and map each one to a particular letter, number, or symbol. The full mapping is called a character set. The most popular character set is commonly referred to as ASCII. The second most popular character set these days is Unicode (and it will probably eventually surpass ASCII). Other fairly common character sets include EBCDIC and PETSCII. They are generally quite different from one another; programs exist to convert between them on most platforms, though. Usually EBCDIC is only found on really old machines.

### CISC
**C**omplex **i**nstruction **s**et **c**omputing is one of the two main types of processor design in use today. It is slowly losing popularity to RISC designs; currently all the fastest processors in the world are RISC. The most popular current CISC processor is the x86, but there are also still some 68xx, 65xx, and Z80s in use.

### CLI
A **c**ommand-**l**ine **i**nterface is a text-based means of communicating with a program, especially an OS. This is the sort of interface used by MS-DOS, or a UNIX shell window.

### COBOL
The **C**ommon **B**usiness **O**riented **L**anguage is a language developed back in 1959 and still used by some businesses. While it is relatively portable, it is still disliked by many professional programmers simply because COBOL programs tend to be physically longer than equivalent programs written in almost any other language in common use.

### compiled
If a program is compiled, its original human-readable source has been converted into a form more easily used by a computer prior to it being run. Such programs will generally run more quickly than interpreted programs, because time was pre-spent in the compilation phase. A program that compiles other programs is called a compiler.

### compression
It is often possible to remove redundant information or capitalize on patterns in data to make a file smaller. Usually when a file has been compressed, it cannot be used until it is uncompressed. Image files are common exceptions, though, as many popular image file formats have compression built-in.

### cookie
A cookie is a small file that a web page on another machine writes to your personal machine's disk to store various bits of information. Many people strongly detest cookies and the whole idea of them, and most browsers allow the reception of cookies to be disabled or at least selectively disabled, but it should be noted that both Netscape and MSIE have silent cookie reception enabled by default. Sites that maintain shopping carts or remember a reader's last position have legitimate uses for cookies. Sites without such functionality that still spew cookies with distant (or worse, non-existent) expiration dates should perhaps be treated with a little caution.

### CP/M
An early DOS for desktops, CP/M runs on both Z80 and the x86 based machines. CP/M provides only a CLI and there really is not any standard way to get a window manager to run on top of it. It is fairly complex and tricky to use. In spite of all this, CP/M was once the most popular DOS and is still in use today.

### crash
If a bug in a program is severe enough, it can cause that program to crash, or to become inoperable without being restarted. On machines that are not multitasking, the entire machine will crash and have to be rebooted. On machines that are only partially multitasking the entire machine will sometimes crash and have to be rebooted. On machines that are fully multitasking, the machine should never crash and require a reboot.

### Cray
A Cray is a high-end computer used for research and frequently heavy-duty graphics applications. Modern Crays typically have Solaris for their OS and sport sixty-four RISC

processors; older ones had various other configurations. Current top-of-the-line Crays can have over 2000 processors.
### crippleware
Crippleware is a variant of shareware that will either self-destruct after its trial period or has built-in limitations to its functionality that get removed after its purchase.
### CSS
Cascading style sheets are used in conjunction with HTML and XHTML to define the layout of web pages. While CSS is how current web pages declare how they should be displayed, it tends not to be supported well (if at all) by ancient browsers. XSL performs this same function more generally.
### desktop publisher
A program for creating newspapers, magazines, books, etc. Some common desktop publishing programs include FrameMaker, PageMaker, InDesign, and GeoPublish.
### DHTML
Dynamic HTML is simply the combined use of both CSS and JavaScript together in the same document; a more extreme form is called AJaX. Note that DHTML is quite different from the similarly named DTML.
### dict
A protocol used for looking up definitions across a network (in particular the Internet).
### digital camera
A digital camera looks and behaves like a regular camera, except instead of using film, it stores the image it sees in memory as a file for later transfer to a computer. Many digital cameras offer additional storage besides their own internal memory; a few sport some sort of disk but the majority utilize some sort of flash card. Digital cameras currently lack the resolution and color palette of real cameras, but are usually much more convenient for computer applications. Another related device is called a scanner.
### DIMM
A physical component used to add RAM to a computer. Similar to, but incompatible with, SIMMs.
### DNS
Domain name service is the means by which a name (like www.saugus.net or ftp.saugus.net) gets converted into a real Internet address that points to a particular machine.
### DoS
In a denial of service attack, many individual (usually compromised) computers are used to try and simultaneously access the same public resource with the intent of overburdening it so that it will not be able to adequately serve its normal users.
### DOS
A disk operating system manages disks and other system resources. Sort of a subset of OSes, sort of an archaic term for the same. MS-DOS is the most popular program currently calling itself a DOS. CP/M was the most popular prior to MS-DOS.
### download
To download a file is to copy it from a remote computer to your own. The opposite is upload.
### DR-DOS
The DOS currently produced by Caldera (originally produced by Design Research as a successor to CP/M) designed to work like MS-DOS. While similar to CP/M in many ways, it utilizes simpler commands. It provides only a CLI, but either Windows 3.1 or GEOS may be run on top of it to provide a GUI. It only runs on x86 based machines.
### driver
A driver is a piece of software that works with the OS to control a particular piece of hardware, like a printer or a scanner or a mouse or whatever.
### DRM

Depending upon whom you ask, DRM can stand for either Digital Rights Management or Digital Restrictions Management. In either case, DRM is used to place restrictions upon the usage of digital media ranging from software to music to video.

**DTML**

The Document Template Mark-up Language is a subset of SGML and a superset of HTML used for creating documents that dynamically adapt to external conditions using its own custom tags and a little bit of Python. Note that it is quite different from the similarly named DHTML.

### EDBIC

The EDBIC character set is similar to (but less popular than) the ASCII character set in concept, but is significantly different in layout. It tends to be found only on old machines..

**emacs**

Emacs is both one of the most powerful and one of the most popular text editing programs in existence. Versions can be found for most platforms, and in fact multiple companies make versions, so for a given platform there might even be a choice. There is even a free GNU version available. The drawback with emacs is that it is not in the least bit lightweight. In fact, it goes so far in the other direction that even its advocates will occasionally joke about it. It is however extremely capable. Almost anything that one would need to relating to text can be done with emacs and is probably built-in. Even if one manages to find something that emacs was not built to do, emacs has a built-in Lisp interpreter capable of not only extending its text editing capabilities, but even of being used as a scripting language in its own right.

**embedded**

An embedded system is a computer that lives inside another device and acts as a component of that device. For example, current cars have an embedded computer under the hood that helps regulate much of their day to day operation.

An embedded file is a file that lives inside another and acts as a portion of that file. This is frequently seen with HTML files having embedded audio files; audio files often embedded in HTML include AU files, MIDI files, SID files, WAV files, AIFF files, and MOD files. Most browsers will ignore these files unless an appropriate plug-in is present.

**emulator**

An emulator is a program that allows one computer platform to mimic another for the purposes of running its software. Typically (but not always) running a program through an emulator will not be quite as pleasant an experience as running it on the real system.

**endian**

A processor will be either "big endian" or "little endian" based upon the manner in which it encodes multiple byte values. There is no difference in performance between the two encoding methods, but it is one of the sources of difficulty when reading binary data on different platforms.

**environment**

An environment (sometimes also called a runtime environment) is a collection of external variable items or parameters that a program can access when run. Information about the computer's hardware and the user can often be found in the environment.

**EPOC**

EPOC is a lightweight OS. It is most commonly found on the Psion PDA.

**extension**

Filename extensions originate back in the days of CP/M and basically allow a very rough grouping of different file types by putting a tag at the end of the name. To further complicate matters, the tag is sometimes separated by the name proper by a period "." and sometimes by a tab. While extensions are semi-enforced on CP/M, MS-DOS, and MS-Windows, they have no real meaning aside from convention on other platforms and are only optional.

**FAQ**

A frequently asked questions file attempts to provide answers for all commonly asked questions related to a given topic.

**FireWire**
An incredibly fast type of serial port that offers many of the best features of SCSI at a lower price. Faster than most types of parallel port, a single FireWire port is capable of chaining many devices without the need of a terminator. FireWire is similar in many respects to USB but is significantly faster and somewhat more expensive. It is heavily used for connecting audio/video devices to computers, but is also used for connecting storage devices like drives and other assorted devices like printers and scanners.

**fixed width**
As applied to a font, fixed width means that every character takes up the same amount of space. That is, an "i" will be just as wide as an "m" with empty space being used for padding. The opposite is variable width. The most common fixed width font is Courier.

**flash**
Flash memory is similar to RAM. It has one significant advantage: it does not lose its contents when power is lost; it has two main disadvantages: it is slower, and it eventually wears out. Flash memory is frequently found in PCMCIA cards.

**font**
In a simplistic sense, a font can be thought of as the physical description of a character set. While the character set will define what sets of bits map to what letters, numbers, and other symbols, the font will define what each letter, number, and other symbol looks like. Fonts can be either fixed width or variable width and independently, either bitmapped or vectored. The size of the large characters in a font is typically measured in points.

**Forth**
A language developed in 1970 by Moore. Forth is fairly portable and has versions on many different platforms. While it is no longer an very popular language, many of its ideas and concepts have been carried into other computer programs. In particular, some programs for doing heavy-duty mathematical and engineering work use Forth-like interfaces.

**FORTRAN**
FORTRAN stands for **formula trans**lation and is the oldest computer language in the world. It is typically compiled and is quite fast. Its primary drawbacks are portability and ease-of-use -- often different FORTRAN compilers on different platforms behave quite differently in spite of standardization efforts in 1966 (FORTRAN 66 or FORTRAN IV), 1978 (FORTRAN 77), and 1991 (FORTRAN 90). Today languages like C and Java are more popular, but FORTRAN is still heavily used in military software. It is somewhat amusing to note that when FORTRAN was first released back in 1958 its advocates thought that it would mean the end of software bugs. In truth of course by making the creation of more complex software practical, computer languages have merely created new types of software bugs.

**FreeBSD**
A free variant of Berkeley UNIX available for Alpha and x86 based machines. It is not as popular as Linux.

**freeware**
Freeware is software that is available for free with no strings attached. The quality is often superb as the authors are also generally users.

**FTP**
The **f**ile **t**ransfer **p**rotocol is one of the most commonly used methods of copying files across the Internet. It has its origins on UNIX machines, but has been adapted to almost every type of computer in existence and is built into many browsers. Most FTP programs have two modes of operation, ASCII, and binary. Transmitting an ASCII file via the ASCII mode of operation is more efficient and cleaner. Transmitting a binary file via the ASCII mode of operation will result in a broken binary file. Thus the FTP programs that do not support both modes of operation will typically only do the binary mode, as binary transfers are capable of transferring both kinds of

data without corruption.
**gateway**
A gateway connects otherwise separate computer networks.
**GEOS**
The **g**raphic **e**nvironment **o**perating **s**ystem is a lightweight OS with a GUI. It runs on several different processors, including the 65xx (different versions for different machines -- there are versions for the C64, the C128, and the Apple ][, each utilizing the relevant custom chip sets), the x86 (although the x86 version is made to run on top of MS-DOS (or PC-DOS or DR-DOS) and is not strictly a full OS or a window manager, rather it is somewhat in between, like Windows 3.1) and numerous different PDAs, embedded devices, and hand-held machines. It was originally designed by Berkeley Softworks (no real relation to the Berkeley of UNIX fame) but is currently in a more interesting state: the company GeoWorks develops and promotes development of GEOS for hand-held devices, PDAs, & and embedded devices and owns (but has ceased further development on) the x86 version. The other versions are owned (and possibly still being developed) by the company CMD.
**GHz & gigahertz**
One gigahertz is equivalent to 1000 megahertz, or 1,000,000,000 hertz.
**Glulx**
A virtual machine optimized for running interactive fiction, interactive tutorials, and other interactive things of a primarily textual nature. Glulx has been ported to several platforms, and in in many ways an upgrade to the Z-machine.
**GNOME**
The **GN**U network **o**bject **m**odel **e**nvironment is a popular free window manager (and much more -- as its name touts, it is more of a desktop environment) that runs under X-Windows. It is a part of the GNU project.
**GNU**
GNU stands for **G**NU's **n**ot **U**NIX and is thus a recursive acronym (and unlike the animal name, the "G" here is pronounced). At any rate, the GNU project is an effort by the Free Software Foundation (FSF) to make all of the traditional UNIX utilities free for whoever wants them. The Free Software Foundation programmers know their stuff, and the quality of the GNU software is on par with the best produced commercially, and often better. All of the GNU software can be downloaded for free or obtained on CD-ROM for a small service fee. Documentation for all GNU software can be downloaded for free or obtained in book form for a small service fee. The Free Software Foundation pays its bills from the collection of service fees and the sale of T-shirts, and exists mostly through volunteer effort. It is based in Cambridge, MA.
**gopher**
Though not as popular as FTP or http, the gopher protocol is implemented by many browsers and numerous other programs and allows the transfer of files across networks. In some respects it can be thought of as a hybrid between FTP and http, although it tends not to be as good at raw file transfer as FTP and is not as flexible as http. The collection of documents available through gopher is often called "gopherspace", and it should be noted that gopherspace is older than the web. It should also be noted that gopher is not getting as much attention as it once did, and surfing through gopherspace is a little like exploring a ghost town, but there is an interesting VR interface available for it, and some things in gopherspace still have not been copied onto the web.
**GUI**
A **g**raphical **u**ser **i**nterface is a graphics-based means of communicating with a program, especially an OS or window manager. In fact, a window manager can be thought of as a GUI for a CLI OS.
**HP-UX**
HP-UX is the version of UNIX designed by Hewlett-Packard to work with their PA-RISC and

68xx based machines.
## HTML
The **H**ypertext **M**ark-up **L**anguage is the language currently most frequently used to express web pages (although it is rapidly being replaced by XHTML). Every browser has the built-in ability to understand HTML. Some browsers can additionally understand Java and browse FTP areas. HTML is a proper subset of SGML.
## http
The **h**ypertext **t**ransfer **p**rotocol is the native protocol of browsers and is most typically used to transfer HTML formatted files. The secure version is called "https".
## Hurd
The Hurd is the official GNU OS. It is still in development and is not yet supported on too many different processors, but promises to be the most powerful OS available. It (like all the GNU software) is free.
## Hz & hertz
Hertz means cycles per second, and makes no assumptions about what is cycling. So, for example, if a fluorescent light flickers once per jiffy, it has a 60 Hz flicker. More typical for computers would be a program that runs once per jiffy and thus has a 60 Hz frequency, or larger units of hertz like kHz, MHz, GHz, or THz.
## i18n
Commonly used to abbreviate the word "internationalization". There are eighteen letters between the "i" and the "n". Similar to (and often used along with) i18n.
## iCalendar
The iCalendar standard refers to the format used to store calendar type information (including events, to-do items, and journal entries) on the Internet. iCalendar data can be found on some World-Wide-Web pages or attached to e-mail messages.
## icon
A small graphical display representing an object, action, or modifier of some sort.
## IDE
Loosely speaking, a disk format sometimes used by MS-Windows, Mac OS, AmigaOS, and (rarely) UNIX. EIDE is enhanced IDE; it is much faster. Generally IDE is inferior (but less expensive) to SCSI, but it varies somewhat with system load and the individual IDE and SCSI components themselves. The quick rundown is that: SCSI-I and SCSI-II will almost always outperform IDE; EIDE will almost always outperform SCSI-I and SCSI-II; SCSI-III and UltraSCSI will almost always outperform EIDE; and heavy system loads give an advantage to SCSI. Note that although loosely speaking it is just a format difference, it is deep down a hardware difference.
## Inform
A compiled, object-oriented language optimized for creating interactive fiction.
## infrared communications
A device with an infrared port can communicate with other devices at a distance by beaming infrared light signals. Two incompatible protocols are used for infrared communications: IrDA and ASK. Many devices support both.
## Instant Messenger
AOL's Instant Messenger is is a means of chatting over the Internet in real-time. It allows both open group discussions and private conversations. Instant Messenger uses a different, proprietary protocol from the more standard IRC, and is not supported on as many platforms.
## interactive fiction
Interactive fiction (often abbreviated "IF" or "I-F") is a form of literature unique to the computer. While the reader cannot influence the direction of a typical story, the reader plays a more active role in an interactive fiction story and completely controls its direction. Interactive fiction works come in all the sizes and genres available to standard fiction, and in fact are not always even

fiction per se (interactive tutorials exist and are slowly becoming more common).
### interpreted
If a program is interpreted, its actual human-readable source is read as it is run by the computer. This is generally a slower process than if the program being run has already been compiled.
### intranet
An intranet is a private network. There are many intranets scattered all over the world. Some are connected to the Internet via gateways.
### IP
IP is the family of protocols that makes up the Internet. The two most common flavors are TCP/IP and UDP/IP.
### IRC
Internet relay chat is a means of chatting over the Internet in real-time. It allows both open group discussions and private conversations. IRC programs are provided by many different companies and will work on many different platforms. AOL's Instant Messenger utilizes a separate incompatible protocol but is otherwise very similar.
### IrDA
The Infrared Data Association (IrDA) is a voluntary organization of various manufacturers working together to ensure that the infrared communications between different computers, PDAs, printers, digital cameras, remote controls, etc. are all compatible with each other regardless of brand. The term is also often used to designate an IrDA compliant infrared communications port on a device. Informally, a device able to communicate via IrDA compliant infrared is sometimes simply said to "have IrDA". There is also an earlier, incompatible, and usually slower type of infrared communications still in use called ASK.
### IRI
An Internationalized Resource Identifier is just a URI with i18n.
### IRIX
The variant of UNIX designed by Silicon Graphics, Inc. IRIX machines are known for their graphics capabilities and were initially optimized for multimedia applications.
### ISDN
An integrated service digital network line can be simply looked at as a digital phone line. ISDN connections to the Internet can be four times faster than the fastest regular phone connection, and because it is a digital connection a modem is not needed. Any computer hooked up to ISDN will typically require other special equipment in lieu of the modem, however. Also, both phone companies and ISPs charge more for ISDN connections than regular modem connections.
### ISP
An Internet service provider is a company that provides Internet support for other entities. AOL (America Online) is a well-known ISP.
### Java
A computer language designed to be both fairly lightweight and extremely portable. It is tightly bound to the web as it is the primary language for web applets. There has also been an OS based on Java for use on small hand-held, embedded, and network computers. It is called JavaOS. Java can be either interpreted or compiled. For web applet use it is almost always interpreted. While its interpreted form tends not to be very fast, its compiled form can often rival languages like C++ for speed. It is important to note however that speed is not Java's primary purpose -- raw speed is considered secondary to portabilty and ease of use.
### JavaScript
JavaScript (in spite of its name) has nothing whatsoever to do with Java (in fact, it's arguably more like Newton Script than Java). JavaScript is an interpreted language built into a browser to provide a relatively simple means of adding interactivity to web pages. It is only supported on a few different browsers, and tends not to work exactly the same on different versions. Thus its

use on the Internet is somewhat restricted to fairly simple programs. On intranets where there are usually fewer browser versions in use, JavaScript has been used to implement much more complex and impressive programs.

**jiffy**
A jiffy is 1/60 of a second. Jiffies are to seconds as seconds are to minutes.

**joystick**
A joystick is a physical device typically used to control objects on a computer screen. It is frequently used for games and sometimes used in place of a mouse.

**JSON**
The JSON is used for data interchange between programs, an area in which the ubiquitous XML is not too well-suited. JSON is lightweight and works extremely cleanly with languages languages including JavaScript, Python, Java, C++, and many others.

**JSON-RPC**
JSON-RPC is like XML-RPC but is significantly more lightweight since it uses JSON in lieu of XML.

**KDE**
The **K** **d**esktop **e**nvironment is a popular free window manager (and much more -- as its name touts, it is more of a desktop environment) that runs under X-Windows.

**Kerberos**
Kerberos is a network authentication protocol. Basically it preserves the integrity of passwords in any untrusted network (like the Internet). Kerberized applications work hand-in-hand with sites that support Kerberos to ensure that passwords cannot be stolen.

**kernel**
The very heart of an OS is often called its kernel. It will usually (at minimum) provide some libraries that give programmers access to its various features.

**kHz & kilohertz**
One kilohertz is equivalent to 1000 hertz. Some older computers have clock speeds measured in kHz.

**l10n**
Commonly used to abbreviate the word "localization". There are ten letters between the "l" and the "n". Similar to (and often used along with) i18n.

**LDAP**
The **L**ightweight **D**irectory **A**ccess **P**rotocol provides a means of sharing address book type of information across an intranet or even across the Internet. Note too that "address book type of information" here is pretty broad; it often includes not just human addresses, but machine addresses, printer configurations, and similar.

**library**
A selection of routines used by programmers to make computers do particular things.

**lightweight**
Something that is lightweight will not consume computer resources (such as RAM and disk space) too much and will thus run on less expensive computer systems.

**Linux**
Believe it or not, one of the fastest, most robust, and powerful multitasking OSes is available for free. Linux can be downloaded for free or be purchased on CD-ROM for a small service charge. A handful of companies distribute Linux including Red Hat, Debian, Caldera, and many others. Linux is also possibly available for more hardware combinations than any other OS (with the possible exception of NetBSD. Supported processors include: Alpha, PowerPC, SPARC, x86, and 68xx. Most processors currently not supported are currently works-in-progress or even available in beta. For example, work is currently underway to provide support for PA-RISC, 65xx, StrongARM, and Z80. People have even successfully gotten Linux working on PDAs. As you may have guessed, Linux can be made quite lightweight. Linux is a variant of UNIX and as

such, most of the traditional UNIX software will run on Linux. This especially includes the GNU software, most of which comes with the majority of Linux distributions. Fast, reliable, stable, and inexpensive, Linux is popular with ISPs, software developers, and home hobbyists alike.

**Lisp**

Lisp stands for **lis**t **p**rocessing and is the second oldest computer language in the world. Being developed in 1959, it lost the title to FORTRAN by only a few months. It is typically interpreted, but compilers are available for some platforms. Attempts were made to standardize the language, and the standard version is called "Common Lisp". There have also been efforts to simplify the language, and the results of these efforts is another language called Scheme. Lisp is a fairly portable language, but is not particularly fast. Today, Lisp is most widely used with AI software.

**load**

There are two popular meanings for load. The first means to fetch some data or a program from a disk and store it in memory. The second indicates the amount of work a component (especially a processor) is being made to do.

**Logo**

Logo is an interpreted language designed by Papert in 1966 to be a tool for helping people (especially kids) learn computer programming concepts. In addition to being used for that purpose, it is often used as a language for controlling mechanical robots and other similar devices. Logo interfaces even exist for building block / toy robot sets. Logo uses a special graphics cursor called "the turtle", and Logo is itself sometimes called "Turtle Graphics". Logo is quite portable but not particularly fast. Versions can be found on almost every computer platform in the world. Additionally, some other languages (notably some Pascal versions) provide Logo-like interfaces for graphics-intensive programming.

**lossy**

If a process is lossy, it means that a little quality is lost when it is performed. If a format is lossy, it means that putting data into that format (or possibly even manipulating it in that format) will cause some slight loss. Lossy processes and formats are typically used for performance or resource utilization reasons. The opposite of lossy is lossless.

**Lua**

Lua is a simple interpreted language. It is extremely portable, and free versions exist for most platforms.

**Mac OS**

Mac OS is the OS used on Macintosh computers. There are two distinctively different versions of it; everything prior to version 10 (sometimes called Mac OS Classic) and everything version 10 or later (called Mac OS X).

**Mac OS Classic**

The OS created by Apple and originally used by Macs is frequently (albeit slightly incorrectly) referred to as Mac OS Classic (officially Mac OS Classic is this original OS running under the modern Mac OS X in emulation. Mac OS combines the functionality of both an OS and a window manager and is often considered to be the easiest OS to use. It is partially multitasking but will still sometimes crash when dealing with a buggy program. It is probably the second most popular OS, next only to Windows 'XP (although it is quickly losing ground to Mac OS X) and has excellent driver support and boasts a fair selection of games. Mac OS will run on PowerPC and 68xx based machines.

**Mac OS X**

Mac OS X (originally called Rhapsody) is the industrial strength OS produced by Apple to run on both PowerPC and x86 systems (replacing what is often referred to as Mac OS Classic. Mac OS X is at its heart a variant of UNIX and possesses its underlying power (and the ability to run many of the traditional UNIX tools, including the GNU tools). It also was designed to mimic other OSes on demand via what it originally refered to as "boxes" (actually high-performance emulators); it has the built-in capability to run programs written for older Mac OS (via its "BlueBox", officially called Mac OS Classic) and work was started on making it also run Windows '95 / '98 / ME software (via what was called its "YellowBox"). There are also a few rumors going around that future versions may even be able to run Newton software (via the "GreenBox"). It provides a selection of two window managers built-in: Aqua and X-Windows (with Aqua being the default).

### machine language
Machine language consists of the raw numbers that can be directly understood by a particular processor. Each processor's machine language will be different from other processors' machine language. Although called "machine language", it is not usually what people think of when talking about computer languages. Machine language dressed up with mnemonics to make it a bit more human-readable is called assembly language.

### Macintosh
A Macintosh (or a Mac for short) is a computer system that has Mac OS for its OS. There are a few different companies that have produced Macs, but by far the largest is Apple. The oldest Macs are based on the 68xx processor; somewhat more recent Macs on the PowerPC processor, and current Macs on the x86 processor. The Macintosh was really the first general purpose computer to employ a GUI.

### MacTel
An x86 based system running some flavor of Mac OS.

### mainframe
A mainframe is any computer larger than a small piece of furniture. A modern mainframe is more powerful than a modern workstation, but more expensive and more difficult to maintain.

### MathML
The **M**ath **M**ark-up **L**anguage is a subset of XML used to represent mathematical formulae and equations. Typically it is found embedded within XHTML documents, although as of this writing not all popular browsers support it.

### megahertz
A million cycles per second, abbreviated MHz. This is often used misleadingly to indicate processor speed, because while one might expect that a higher number would indicate a faster processor, that logic only holds true within a given type of processors as different types of processors are capable of doing different amounts of work within a cycle. For a current example, either a 200 MHz PowerPC or a 270 MHz SPARC will outperform a 300 MHz Pentium.

### Merced
The Merced is a RISC processor developed by Intel with help from Hewlett-Packard and possibly Sun. It is just starting to be released, but is intended to eventually replace both the x86 and PA-RISC processors. Curiously, HP is recommending that everyone hold off using the first release and instead wait for the second one. It is expected some day to be roughly as fast as an Alpha or PowerPC. It is expected to be supported by future versions of Solaris, Windows-NT, HP-UX, Mac OS X, and Linux. The current semi-available Merced processor is called the Itanium. Its overall schedule is way behind, and some analysts predict that it never will really be released in significant quanitities.

### MFM
Loosely speaking, An old disk format sometimes used by CP/M, MS-DOS, and MS-Windows. No longer too common as it cannot deliver close to the performance of either SCSI or IDE.

### middleware
Software designed to sit in between an OS and applications. Common examples are Java and Tcl/Tk.

### MIME
The **m**ulti-purpose **I**nternet **m**ail **e**xtensions specification describes a means of sending non-

ASCII data (such as images, sounds, foreign symbols, etc.) through e-mail. It commonly utilizes bcode.

**MMX**
**M**ulti**m**edia e**x**tensions were built into some x86 CPUs to provide better performance for certain operations, most notably graphics and sound. It is similar to AltiVec on the PowerPC CPUs. Like AltiVec, it requires special software for full performance benefits to be realized.

**MOB**
A **mo**vable **ob**ject is a graphical object that is manipulated separately from the background. These are seen all the time in computer games. When implemented in hardware, MOBs are sometimes called sprites.

**Modula-2 & Modula-3**
Modula-2 is a procedural language based on Pascal by its original author in around the 1977 - 1979 time period. Modula-3 is an intended successor that adds support for object-oriented constructs (among other things). Modula-2 can be either compiled or interpreted, while Modula-3 tends to be just a compiled language.

**MOTD**
A **m**essage **o**f **t**he **d**ay. Many computers (particularly more capable ones) are configured to display a MOTD when accessed remotely.

**Motif**
Motif is a popular commercial window manager that runs under X-Windows. Free work-alike versions are also available.

**MS-DOS**
The DOS produced by Microsoft. Early versions of it bear striking similarities to the earlier CP/M, but it utilizes simpler commands. It provides only a CLI, but either OS/2, Windows 3.1, Windows '95, Windows '98, Windows ME, or GEOS may be run on top of it to provide a GUI. It only runs on x86 based machines.

**MS-Windows**
MS-Windows is the name collectively given to several somewhat incompatible OSes all produced by Microsoft. They are: Windows CE, Windows NT, Windows 3.1, Windows '95, Windows '98, Windows ME, Windows 2000, and Windows XP.

**MUD**
A **m**ulti-**u**ser **d**imension (also sometimes called multi-user dungeon, but in either case abbreviated to "MUD") is sort of a combination between the online chatting abilities provided by something like IRC and a role-playing game. A MUD built with object oriented principles in mind is called a "Multi-user dimension object-oriented", or MOO. Yet another variant is called a "multi-user shell", or MUSH. Still other variants are called multi-user role-playing environments (MURPE) and multi-user environments (MUSE). There are probably more. In all cases the differences will be mostly academic to the regular user, as the same software is used to connect to all of them. Software to connect to MUDs can be found for most platforms, and there are even Java based ones that can run from within a browser.

**multitasking**
Some OSes have built into them the ability to do several things at once. This is called multitasking, and has been in use since the late sixties / early seventies. Since this ability is built into the software, the overall system will be slower running two things at once than it will be running just one thing. A system may have more than one processor built into it though, and such a system will be capable of running multiple things at once with less of a performance hit.

**nagware**
Nagware is a variant of shareware that will frequently remind its users to register.

**NetBSD**
A free variant of Berkeley UNIX available for Alpha, x86, 68xx, PA-RISC, SPARC, PowerPC, ARM, and many other types of machines. Its emphasis is on portability.

**netiquette**
The established conventions of online politeness are called netiquette. Some conventions vary from site to site or online medium to online medium; others are pretty standard everywhere. Newbies are often unfamiliar with the conventional rules of netiquette and sometimes embarrass themselves accordingly. Be sure not to send that incredibly important e-mail message before reading about netiquette.

**newbie**
A newbie is a novice to the online world or computers in general.

**news**
Usenet news can generally be thought of as public e-mail as that is generally the way it behaves. In reality, it is implemented by different software and is often accessed by different programs. Different newsgroups adhere to different topics, and some are "moderated", meaning that humans will try to manually remove off-topic posts, especially spam. Most established newsgroups have a FAQ, and people are strongly encouraged to read the FAQ prior to posting.

**Newton**
Although Newton is officially the name of the lightweight OS developed by Apple to run on its MessagePad line of PDAs, it is often used to mean the MessagePads (and compatible PDAs) themselves and thus the term "Newton OS" is often used for clarity. The Newton OS is remarkably powerful; it is fully multitasking in spite of the fact that it was designed for small machines. It is optimized for hand-held use, but will readily transfer data to all manner of desktop machines. Historically it was the first PDA. Recently Apple announced that it will discontinue further development of the Newton platform, but will instead work to base future hand-held devices on either Mac OS or Mac OS X with some effort dedicated to making the new devices capable of running current Newton programs.

**Newton book**
Newton books provide all the functionality of ordinary books but add searching and hypertext capabilities. The format was invented for the Newton to provide a means of making volumes of data portable, and is particularly popular in the medical community as most medical references are available as Newton books and carrying around a one pound Newton is preferable to carrying around twenty pounds of books, especially when it comes to looking up something. In addition to medical books, numerous references, most of the classics, and many contemporary works of fiction are available as Newton books. Most fiction is available for free, most references cost money. Newton books are somewhat more capable than the similar Palm DOC; both are specific types of e-books.

**Newton Script**
A intepreted, object-oriented language for Newton MessagePad computers.

**nybble**
A nybble is half a byte, or four bits. It is a case of computer whimsy; it only stands to reason that a small byte should be called a nybble. Some authors spell it with an "i" instead of the "y", but the "y" is the original form.

**object-oriented**
While the specifics are well beyond the scope of this document, the term "object-oriented" applies to a philosophy of software creation. Often this philosophy is referred to as object-oriented design (sometimes abbreviated as OOD), and programs written with it in mind are referred to as object-oriented programs (often abbreviated OOP). Programming languages designed to help facilitate it are called object-oriented languages (sometimes abbreviated as OOL) and databases built with it in mind are called object-oriented databases (sometimes abbreviated as OODB or less fortunately OOD). The general notion is that an object-oriented approach to creating software starts with modeling the real-world problems trying to be solved in familiar real-world ways, and carries the analogy all the way down to structure of the program. This is of course a great over-simplification. Numerous object-oriented programming languages

exist including: Java, C++, Modula-2, Newton Script, and ADA.

**Objective-C & ObjC**

Objective-C (often called "ObjC" for short) is a compiled object-oriented language. Based heavily on C, Objective-C is nearly as fast and can often be thought of as being just C with added features. Note that it was developed independently of C++; its object-oriented extensions are more in the style of Smalltalk. It is however related to Objective-C++.

**Objective-C++ & ObjC++**

Objective-C++ (often called "ObjC++" for short) is a curious hybrid of Objective-C and C++, allowing the syntax of both to coexist in the same source files.

**office suite**

An office suite is a collection of programs including at minimum a word processor, spreadsheet, drawing program, and minimal database program. Some common office suites include MS-Office, AppleWorks, ClarisWorks, GeoWorks, Applixware, Corel Office, and StarOffice.

**open source**

Open source software goes one step beyond freeware. Not only does it provide the software for free, it provides the original source code used to create the software. Thus, curious users can poke around with it to see how it works, and advanced users can modify it to make it work better for them. By its nature, open souce software is pretty well immune to all types of computer virus.

**OpenBSD**

A free variant of Berkeley UNIX available for Alpha, x86, 68xx, PA-RISC, SPARC, and PowerPC based machines. Its emphasis is on security.

**OpenDocument & ODF**

OpenDocument (or ODF for short) is the suite of open, XML-based office suite application formats defined by the OASIS consortium. It defines a platform-neutral, non-proprietary way of storing documents.

**OpenGL**

A low-level 3D graphics library with an emphasis on speed developed by SGI.

**OS/2**

OS/2 is the OS designed by IBM to run on x86 based machines. It is semi-compatible with MS-Windows. IBM's more industrial strength OS is called AIX.

**PA-RISC**

The PA-RISC is a RISC processor developed by Hewlett-Packard. It is currently produced only by HP. At the moment only one OS runs on PA-RISC based machines: HP-UX. There is an effort underway to port Linux to them, though.

**Palm DOC**

Palm DOC files are quite similar to (but slightly less capable than) Newton books. They were designed for Palm Pilots but can now be read on a couple other platforms, too. They are a specific type of e-book.

**Palm Pilot**

The Palm Pilot (also called both just Palm and just Pilot, officially now just Palm) is the most popular PDA currently in use. It is one of the least capable PDAs, but it is also one of the smallest and least expensive. While not as full featured as many of the other PDAs (such as the Newton) it performs what features it does have quite well and still remains truly pocket-sized.

**parallel**

Loosely speaking, parallel implies a situation where multiple things can be done simultaneously, like having multiple check-out lines each serving people all at once. Parallel connections are by their nature more expensive than serial ones, but usually faster. Also, in a related use of the word, often multitasking computers are said to be capable of running multiple programs in parallel.

**partition**

Sometimes due to hardware limitations, disks have to be divided into smaller pieces. These

pieces are called partitions.
## Pascal
Named after the mathematician Blaise Pascal, Pascal is a language designed by Niklaus Wirth originally in 1968 (and heavily revised in 1972) mostly for purposes of education and training people how to write computer programs. It is a typically compiled language but is still usually slower than C or FORTRAN. Wirth also created a more powerful object-oriented Pascal-like language called Modula-2.
## PC-DOS
The DOS produced by IBM designed to work like MS-DOS. Early versions of it bear striking similarities to the earlier CP/M, but it utilizes simpler commands. It provides only a CLI, but either Windows 3.1 or GEOS may be run on top of it to provide a GUI. It only runs on x86 based machines.
## PCMCIA
The **P**ersonal **C**omputer **M**emory **C**ard **I**nternational **A**ssociation is a standards body that concern themselves with PC Card technology. Often the PC Cards themselves are referred to as "PCMCIA cards". Frequently flash memory can be found in PC card form.
## Perl
Perl is an interpreted language extremely popular for web applications.
## PET
The Commodore PET (**P**ersonal **E**lectronic **T**ransactor) is an early (circa 1977-1980, around the same time as the Apple][) home computer featuring a ROM-based BASIC developed by Microsoft which it uses as a default "OS". It is based on the 65xx family of processors and is the precursor to the VIC-20.
## PETSCII
The PETSCII character set gets its name from "**PET AS**CII; it is a variant of the ASCII character set originally developed for the Commodore PET that swaps the upper and lower case characters and adds over a hundred graphic characters in addition to other small changes. If you encounter some text that seems to have uppercase where lowercase is expected and vice-versa, it is probably a PETSCII file.
## PHP
Named with a recursive acronym (PHP: Hypertext Preprocessor), PHP provides a means of creating web pages that dynamically modify themselves on the fly.
## ping
Ping is a protocol designed to check across a network to see if a particular computer is "alive" or not. Computers that recognize the ping will report back their status. Computers that are down will not report back anything at all.
## pixel
The smallest distinct point on a computer display is called a pixel.
## plug-in
A plug-in is a piece of software designed not to run on its own but rather work in cooperation with a separate application to increase that application's abilities.
## point
There are two common meanings for this word. The first is in the geometric sense; a position in space without size. Of course as applied to computers it must take up some space in practise (even if not in theory) and it is thus sometimes synonomous with pixel. The other meaning is related most typically to fonts and regards size. The exact meaning of it in this sense will unfortunately vary somewhat from person to person, but will often mean 1/72 of an inch. Even when it does not exactly mean 1/72 of an inch, larger point sizes always indicate larger fonts.
## PowerPC
The PowerPC is a RISC processor developed in a collaborative effort between IBM, Apple, and Motorola. It is currently produced by a few different companies, of course including its original

developers. A few different OSes run on PowerPC based machines, including Mac OS, AIX, Solaris, Windows NT, Linux, Mac OS X, BeOS, and AmigaOS. At any given time, the fastest processor in the world is usually either a PowerPC or an Alpha, but sometimes SPARCs and PA-RISCs make the list, too.

**proprietary**
This simply means to be supplied by only one vendor. It is commonly misused. Currently, most processors are non-proprietary, some systems are non-proprietary, and every OS (except for arguably Linux) is proprietary.

**protocol**
A protocol is a means of communication used between computers. As long as both computers recognize the same protocol, they can communicate without too much difficulty over the same network or even via a simple direct modem connection regardless whether or not they are themselves of the same type. This means that WinTel boxes, Macs, Amigas, UNIX machines, etc., can all talk with one another provided they agree on a common protocol first.

**Psion**
The Psion is a fairly popular brand of PDA. Generally, it is in between a Palm and a Newton in capability. It runs the EPOC OS.

**Python**
Python is an interpreted, object-oriented language popular for Internet applications. It is extremely portable with free versions existing for virtually every platform.

**queue**
A queue is a waiting list of things to be processed. Many computers provide printing queues, for example. If something is being printed and the user requests that another item be printed, the second item will sit in the printer queue until the first item finishes printing at which point it will be removed from the queue and get printed itself.

**QuickDraw**
A high-level 3D graphics library with an emphasis on quick development time created by Apple.

**RAM**
**R**andom **a**ccess **m**emory is the short-term memory of a computer. Any information stored in RAM will be lost if power goes out, but the computer can read from RAM far more quickly than from a drive.

**random access**
Also called "dynamic access" this indicates that data can be selected without having to skip over earlier data first. This is the way that a CD, record, laserdisc, or DVD will behave -- it is easy to selectively play a particular track without having to fast forward through earlier tracks. The other common behavior is called sequential access.

**RDF**
The **R**esource **D**escription **F**ramework is built upon an XML base and provides a more modern means of accessing data from Internet resources. It can provide metadata (including annotations) for web pages making (among other things) searching more capable. It is also being used to refashion some existing formats like RSS and iCalendar; in the former case it is already in place (at least for newer RSS versions), but it is still experimental in the latter case.

**real-time**
Something that happens in real-time will keep up with the events around it and never give any sort of "please wait" message.

**Rexx**
The **R**estructured **Ex**tended **Ex**ecutor is an interpreted language designed primarily to be embedded in other applications in order to make them consistently programmable, but also to be easy to learn and understand.

**RISC**
**R**educed **i**nstruction **s**et **c**omputing is one of the two main types of processor design in use

today, the other being CISC. The fastest processors in the world today are all RISC designs. There are several popular RISC processors, including Alphas, ARMs, PA-RISCs, PowerPCs, and SPARCs.

**robot**
A robot (or 'bot for short) in the computer sense is a program designed to automate some task, often just sending messages or collecting information. A spider is a type of robot designed to traverse the web performing some task (usually collecting data).

**robust**
The adjective robust is used to describe programs that are better designed, have fewer bugs, and are less likely to crash.

**ROM**
Read-only memory is similar to RAM only cannot be altered and does not lose its contents when power is removed.

**RSS**
RSS stands for either Rich Site Summary, Really Simple Syndication, or RDF Site Summary, depending upon whom you ask. The general idea is that it can provide brief summaries of articles that appear in full on a web site. It is well-formed XML, and newer versions are even more specifically well-formed RDF.

**Ruby**
Ruby is an interpreted, object-oriented language. Ruby was fairly heavily influenced by Perl, so people familiar with that language can typically transition to Ruby easily.

**scanner**
A scanner is a piece of hardware that will examine a picture and produce a computer file that represents what it sees. A digital camera is a related device. Each has its own limitations.

**Scheme**
Scheme is a typically interpreted computer language. It was created in 1975 in an attempt to make Lisp simpler and more consistent. Scheme is a fairly portable language, but is not particularly fast.

**script**
A script is a series of OS commands. The term "batch file" means much the same thing, but is a bit dated. Typically the same sort of situations in which one would say DOS instead of OS, it would also be appropriate to say batch file instead of script. Scripts can be run like programs, but tend to perform simpler tasks. When a script is run, it is always interpreted.

**SCSI**
Loosely speaking, a disk format sometimes used by MS-Windows, Mac OS, AmigaOS, and (almost always) UNIX. Generally SCSI is superior (but more expensive) to IDE, but it varies somewhat with system load and the individual SCSI and IDE components themselves. The quick rundown is that: SCSI-I and SCSI-II will almost always outperform IDE; EIDE will almost always outperform SCSI-I and SCSI-II; SCSI-III and UltraSCSI will almost always outperform EIDE; and heavy system loads give an advantage to SCSI. Note that although loosely speaking it is just a format difference, it is deep down a hardware difference.

**sequential access**
This indicates that data cannot be selected without having to skip over earlier data first. This is the way that a cassette or video tape will behave. The other common behavior is called random access.

**serial**
Loosely speaking, serial implies something that has to be done linearly, one at a time, like people being served in a single check-out line. Serial connections are by their nature less expensive than parallel connections (including things like SCSI) but are typically slower.

**server**
A server is a computer designed to provide various services for an entire network. It is typically

either a workstation or a mainframe because it will usually be expected to handle far greater loads than ordinary desktop systems. The load placed on servers also necessitates that they utilize robust OSes, as a crash on a system that is currently being used by many people is far worse than a crash on a system that is only being used by one person.

**SGML**
The **S**tandard **G**eneralized **M**ark-up **L**anguage provides an extremely generalized level of mark-up. More common mark-up languages like HTML and XML are actually just popular subsets of SGML.

**shareware**
Shareware is software made for profit that allows a trial period before purchase. Typically shareware can be freely downloaded, used for a period of weeks (or sometimes even months), and either purchased or discarded after it has been learned whether or not it will satisfy the user's needs.

**shell**
A CLI designed to simplify complex OS commands. Some OSes (like AmigaOS, the Hurd, and UNIX) have built-in support to make the concurrent use of multiple shells easy. Common shells include the Korn Shell (ksh), the Bourne Shell (sh or bsh), the Bourne-Again Shell, (bash or bsh), the C-Shell (csh), etc.

**SIMM**
A physical component used to add RAM to a computer. Similar to, but incompatible with, DIMMs.

**Smalltalk**
Smalltalk is an efficient language for writing computer programs. Historically it is one of the first object-oriented languages, and is not only used today in its pure form but shows its influence in other languages like Objective-C.

**Solaris**
Solaris is the commercial variant of UNIX currently produced by Sun. It is an industrial strength, nigh bulletproof, powerful multitasking OS that will run on SPARC, x86, and PowerPC based machines.

**spam**
Generally spam is unwanted, unrequested e-mail or Usenet news. It is typically sent out in bulk to huge address lists that were automatically generated by various robots endlessly searching the Internet and newsgroups for things that resemble e-mail addresses. The legality of spam is a topic of much debate; it is at best only borderline legal, and spammers have been successfully persecuted in some states.

**SPARC**
The SPARC is a RISC processor developed by Sun. The design was more or less released to the world, and it is currently produced by around a dozen different companies too numerous to even bother mentioning. It is worth noting that even computers made by Sun typically sport SPARCs made by other companies. A couple different OSes run on SPARC based machines, including Solaris, SunOS, and Linux. Some of the newer SPARC models are called UltraSPARCs.

**sprite**
The term sprite originally referred to a small MOB, usually implemented in hardware. Lately it is also being used to refer to a single image used piecemeal within a Web site in order to avoid incurring the time penalty of downloading multiple files.

**SQL**
SQL (pronounced **Sequel**) is an interpreted language specially designed for database access. It is supported by virtually every major modern database system.

**Sugar**
The window manager used by the OLPC XO. It is made to run on top of Linux.

### SunOS
SunOS is the commercial variant of UNIX formerly produced (but still supported) by Sun.
### SVG
**S**calable **V**ector **G**raphics data is an XML file that is used to hold graphical data that can be resized without loss of quality. SVG data can be kept in its own file, or even embedded within a web page (although not all browsers are capable of displaying such data).
### Tcl/Tk
The **T**ool **C**ommand **L**anguage is a portable interpreted computer language designed to be easy to use. Tk is a GUI toolkit for Tcl. Tcl is a fairly popular language for both integrating existing applications and for creating Web applets (note that applets written in Tcl are often called Tcklets). Tcl/Tk is available for free for most platforms, and plug-ins are available to enable many browsers to play Tcklets.
### TCP/IP
TCP/IP is a protocol for computer networks. The Internet is largely built on top of TCP/IP (it is the more reliable of the two primary **I**nternet **P**rotocols -- TCP stands for **T**ransmission **C**ontrol **P**rotocol).
### terminator
A terminator is a dedicated device used to mark the end of a device chain (as is most typically found with SCSI devices). If such a chain is not properly terminated, weird results can occur.
### TEX
TEX (pronounced "tek") is a freely available, industrial strength typesetting program that can be run on many different platforms. These qualities make it exceptionally popular in schools, and frequently software developed at a university will have its documentation in TEX format. TEX is not limited to educational use, though; many professional books were typeset with TEX. TEX's primary drawback is that it can be quite difficult to set up initially.
### THz & terahertz
One terahertz is equivalent to 1000 gigahertz.
### TrackBack
TrackBacks essentially provide a means whereby different web sites can post messages to one another not just to inform each other about citations, but also to alert one another of related resources. Typically, a blog may display quotations from another blog through the use of TrackBacks.
### UDP/IP
UDP/IP is a protocol for computer networks. It is the faster of the two primary **I**nternet **P**rotocols. UDP stands for **U**ser **D**atagram **P**rotocol.
### Unicode
The Unicode character set is a superset of the ASCII character set with provisions made for handling international symbols and characters from other languages. Unicode is sixteen bit, so takes up roughly twice the space as simple ASCII, but is correspondingly more flexible.
### UNIX
UNIX is a family of OSes, each being made by a different company or organization but all offering a very similar look and feel. It can not quite be considered non-proprietary, however, as the differences between different vendor's versions can be significant (it is still generally possible to switch from one vendor's UNIX to another without too much effort; today the differences between different UNIXes are similar to the differences between the different MS-Windows; historically there were two different UNIX camps, Berkeley / BSD and AT&T / System V, but the assorted vendors have worked together to minimalize the differences). The free variant Linux is one of the closest things to a current, non-proprietary OS; its development is controlled by a non-profit organization and its distribution is provided by several companies. UNIX is powerful; it is fully multitasking and can do pretty much anything that any OS can do (look to the Hurd if you need a more powerful OS). With power comes complexity, however, and

UNIX tends not to be overly friendly to beginners (although those who think UNIX is difficult or cryptic apparently have not used CP/M). Window managers are available for UNIX (running under X-Windows) and once properly configured common operations will be almost as simple on a UNIX machine as on a Mac. Out of all the OSes in current use, UNIX has the greatest range of hardware support. It will run on machines built around many different processors. Lightweight versions of UNIX have been made to run on PDAs, and in the other direction, full featured versions make full advantage of all the resources on large, multi-processor machines. Some different UNIX versions include Solaris, Linux, IRIX, AIX, SunOS, FreeBSD, Digital UNIX, HP-UX, NetBSD, OpenBSD, etc.

**upload**
To upload a file is to copy it from your computer to a remote computer. The opposite is download.

**UPS**
An **u**ninterrupted **p**ower **s**upply uses heavy duty batteries to help smooth out its input power source.

**URI**
A **U**niform **R**esource **I**dentifier is basically just a unique address for almost any type of resource. It is similar to but more general than a URL; in fact, it may also be a URN.

**URL**
A **U**niform **R**esource **L**ocator is basically just an address for a file that can be given to a browser. It starts with a protocol type (such as http, ftp, or gopher) and is followed by a colon, machine name, and file name in UNIX style. Optionally an octothorpe character "#" and and arguments will follow the file name; this can be used to further define position within a page and perform a few other tricks. Similar to but less general than a URI.

**URN**
A **U**niform **R**esource **N**ame is basically just a unique address for almost any type of resource unlike a URL it will probably not resolve with a browser.

**USB**
A really fast type of serial port that offers many of the best features of SCSI without the price. Faster than many types of parallel port, a single USB port is capable of chaining many devices without the need of a terminator. USB is much slower (but somewhat less expensive) than FireWire.

**uucode**
The point of uucode is to allow 8-bit binary data to be transferred through the more common 7-bit ASCII channels (most especially e-mail). The facilities for dealing with uucoded files exist for many different machine types, and the most common programs are called "uuencode" for encoding the original binary file into a 7-bit file and "uudecode" for restoring the original binary file from the encoded one. Sometimes different uuencode and uudecode programs will work in subtly different manners causing annoying compatibility problems. Bcode was invented to provide the same service as uucode but to maintain a tighter standard.

**variable width**
As applied to a font, variable width means that different characters will have different widths as appropriate. For example, an "i" will take up much less space than an "m". The opposite of variable width is fixed width. The terms "proportional width" and "proportionally spaced" mean the same thing as variable width. Some common variable width fonts include Times, Helvetica, and Bookman.

**VAX**
The VAX is a computer platform developed by Digital. Its plural is VAXen. VAXen are large expensive machines that were once quite popular in large businesses; today modern UNIX workstations have all the capability of VAXen but take up much less space. Their OS is called VMS.

**vector**
This term has two common meanings. The first is in the geometric sense: a vector defines a direction and magnitude. The second concerns the formatting of fonts and images. If a font is a vector font or an image is a vector image, it is defined as lines of relative size and direction rather than as collections of pixels (the method used in bitmapped fonts and images). This makes it easier to change the size of the font or image, but puts a bigger load on the device that has to display the font or image. The term "outline font" means the same thing as vector font.

**Veronica & Veronica2**
Although traditionally written as a proper name, Veronica is actually an acronym for "**v**ery **e**asy **r**odent-**o**riented **n**etwide **i**ndex to **c**omputerized **a**rchives", where the "rodent" refers to gopher. The acronym was obviously a little forced to go along with the pre-existing (and now largely unused) Archie, in order to have a little fun with a comic book reference. Regardless, Veronica (or these days more likely Veronica2) is essentially a search engine for gopher resources.

**VIC-20**
The Commodore VIC-20 computer sold millions of units and is generally considered to have been the first affordable home computer. It features a ROM-based BASIC and uses it as a default "OS". It is based on the 65xx family of processors. VIC (in case you are wondering) can stand for either **v**ideo **i**nterface **c** or **v**ideo **i**nterface **c**omputer. The VIC-20 is the precursor to the C64/128.

**virtual machine**
A virtual machine is a machine completely defined and implemented in software rather than hardware. It is often referred to as a "runtime environment"; code compiled for such a machine is typically called bytecode.

**virtual memory**
This is a scheme by which disk space is made to substitute for the more expensive RAM space. Using it will often enable a comptuer to do things it could not do without it, but it will also often result in an overall slowing down of the system. The concept of swap space is very similar.

**virtual reality**
Virtual reality (often called VR for short) is generally speaking an attempt to provide more natural, human interfaces to software. It can be as simple as a pseudo 3D interface or as elaborate as an isolated room in which the computer can control the user's senses of vision, hearing, and even smell and touch.

**virus**
A virus is a program that will seek to duplicate itself in memory and on disks, but in a subtle way that will not immediately be noticed. A computer on the same network as an infected computer or that uses an infected disk (even a floppy) or that downloads and runs an infected program can itself become infected. A virus can only spread to computers of the same platform. For example, on a network consisting of a WinTel box, a Mac, and a Linux box, if one machine acquires a virus the other two will probably still be safe. Note also that different platforms have different general levels of resistance; UNIX machines are almost immune, Win '95 / '98 / ME / XP is quite vulnerable, and most others lie somewhere in between.

**VMS**
The industrial strength OS that runs on VAXen.

**VoIP**
VoIP means "Voice over IP" and it is quite simply a way of utilizing the Internet (or even in some cases intranets) for telephone conversations. The primary motivations for doing so are cost and convenience as VoIP is significantly less expensive than typical telephone long distance packages, plus one high speed Internet connection can serve for multiple phone lines.

**VRML**
A **V**irtual **R**eality **M**odeling **L**anguage file is used to represent VR objects. It has essentially been superceded by X3D.

**W3C**
The World Wide Web Consortium (usually abbreviated W3C) is a non-profit, advisory body that makes suggestions on the future direction of the World Wide Web, HTML, CSS, and browsers.
**Waba**
An extremely lightweight subset of Java optimized for use on PDAs.
**WebDAV**
WebDAV stands for Web-based Distributed Authoring and Versioning, and is designed to provide a way of editing Web-based resources in place. It serves as a more modern (and often more secure) replacement for FTP in many cases.
**WebTV**
A WebTV box hooks up to an ordinary television set and displays web pages. It will not display them as well as a dedicated computer.
**window manager**
A window manager is a program that acts as a graphical go-between for a user and an OS. It provides a GUI for the OS. Some OSes incorporate the window manager into their own internal code, but many do not for reasons of efficiency. Some OSes partially make the division. Some common true window managers include CDE (Common Desktop Environment), GNOME, KDE, Aqua, OpenWindows, Motif, FVWM, Sugar, and Enlightenment. Some common hybrid window managers with OS extensions include Windows ME, Windows 98, Windows 95, Windows 3.1, OS/2 and GEOS.
**Windows '95**
Windows '95 is currently the second most popular variant of MS-Windows. It was designed to be the replacement Windows 3.1 but has not yet done so completely partly because of suspected security problems but even more because it is not as lightweight and will not work on all the machines that Windows 3.1 will. It is more capable than Windows 3.1 though and now has excellent driver support and more games available for it than any other platform. It is made to run on top of MS-DOS and will not do much of anything if MS-DOS is not on the system. It is thus not strictly an OS per se, but nor is it a true window manager either; rather the combination of MS-DOS and Windows '95 result in a full OS with GUI. It is partially multitasking but has a much greater chance of crashing than Windows NT does (or probably even Mac OS) if faced with a buggy program. Windows '95 runs only on x86 based machines. Currently Windows '95 has several Y2K issues, some of which have patches that can be downloaded for free, and some of which do not yet have fixes at all.
**Windows '98**
Windows '98 is quite possibly the second most popular form of MS-Windows, in spite of the fact that its official release is currently a point of legal debate with at least nineteen states, the federal government, and a handful of foreign countries as it has a few questionable features that might restrict the novice computer user and/or unfairly compete with other computer companies. It also has some specific issues with the version of Java that comes prepackaged with it that has never been adequately fixed, and it still has several Y2K issues, most of which have patches that can be downloaded for free (in fact, Microsoft guarantees that it will work properly through 2000 with the proper patches), but some of which do not yet have fixes at all (it won't work properly through 2001 at this point). In any case, it was designed to replace Windows '95.
**Windows 2000**
Windows 2000 was the intended replacement for Windows NT and in that capacity received relatively lukewarm support. Being based on Windows NT, it inherits some of its driver support problems. Originally it was also supposed to replace Windows '98, but Windows ME was made to do that instead, and the merger between Windows NT and Windows '98 was postponed until Windows XP.
**Windows 3.1**
Windows 3.1 remains a surprisingly popular variant of MS-Windows. It is lighter weight than

either Windows '95 or Windows NT (but not lighter weight than GEOS) but less capable than the other two. It is made to run on top of MS-DOS and will not do much of anything if MS-DOS is not on the system. It is thus not strictly an OS per se, but nor is it a true window manager, either; rather the combination of MS-DOS and Windows 3.1 result in a full OS with GUI. Its driver support is good, but its game selection is limited. Windows 3.1 runs only on x86 based machines. It has some severe Y2K issues that may or may not be fixed.

**Windows CE**

Windows CE is the lightweight variant of MS-Windows. It offers the general look and feel of Windows '95 but is targetted primarily for hand-held devices, PDAs, NCs, and embedded devices. It does not have all the features of either Windows '95 or Windows NT and is very different from Windows 3.1. In particular, it will not run any software made for any of the other versions of MS-Windows. Special versions of each program must be made. Furthermore, there are actually a few slightly different variants of Windows CE, and no variant is guaranteed to be able to run software made specifically for another one. Driver support is also fairly poor for all types, and few games are made for it. Windows CE will run on a few different processor types, including the x86 and several different processors dedicated to PDAs, embedded systems, and hand-held devices.

**Windows ME**

Windows ME is yet another flavor of MS-Windows (specifically the planned replacement for Windows '98). Windows ME currently runs only on the x86 processor.

**Windows NT**

Windows NT is the industrial-strength variant of MS-Windows. Current revisions offer the look and feel of Windows '95 and older revisions offer the look and feel of Windows 3.1. It is the most robust flavor of MS-Windows and is fully multitasking. It is also by far the most expensive flavor of MS-Windows and has far less software available for it than Windows '95 or '98. In particular, do not expect to play many games on a Windows NT machine, and expect some difficulty in obtaining good drivers. Windows NT will run on a few different processor types, including the x86, the Alpha, and the PowerPC. Plans are in place to port Windows NT to the Merced when it becomes available.

**Windows Vista**

Windows Vista is the newest flavor of MS-Windows (specifically the planned replacement for Windows XP). Windows Vista (originally known as Longhorn) currently only runs on x86 processors.

**Windows XP**

Windows XP is yet another flavor of MS-Windows (specifically the planned replacement for both Windows ME and Windows 2000). Windows XP currently only runs on the x86 processors. Windows XP is currently the most popular form of MS-Windows.

**WinTel**

An x86 based system running some flavor of MS-Windows.

**workstation**

Depending upon whom you ask, a workstation is either an industrial strength desktop computer or its own category above the desktops. Workstations typically have some flavor of UNIX for their OS, but there has been a recent trend to call high-end Windows NT and Windows 2000 machines workstations, too.

**WYSIWYG**

What you see is what you get; an adjective applied to a program that attempts to exactly represent printed output on the screen. Related to WYSIWYM but quite different.

**WYSIWYM**

What you see is what you mean; an adjective applied to a program that does not attempt to exactly represent printed output on the screen, but rather defines how things are used and so will adapt to different paper sizes, etc. Related to WYSIWYG but quite different.

**X-Face**
X-Faces are small monochrome images embedded in headers for both provides a e-mail and news messages. Better mail and news applications will display them (sometimes automatically, sometimes only per request).
**X-Windows**
X-Windows provides a GUI for most UNIX systems, but can also be found as an add-on library for other computers. Numerous window managers run on top of it. It is often just called "X".
**X3D**
Extensible 3D Graphics data is an XML file that is used to hold three-dimensional graphical data. It is the successor to VRML.
**x86**
The x86 series of processors includes the Pentium, Pentium Pro, Pentium II, Pentium III, Celeron, and Athlon as well as the 786, 686, 586, 486, 386, 286, 8086, 8088, etc. It is an exceptionally popular design (by far the most popular CISC series) in spite of the fact that even its fastest model is significantly slower than the assorted RISC processors. Many different OSes run on machines built around x86 processors, including MS-DOS, Windows 3.1, Windows '95, Windows '98, Windows ME, Windows NT, Windows 2000, Windows CE, Windows XP, GEOS, Linux, Solaris, OpenBSD, NetBSD, FreeBSD, Mac OS X, OS/2, BeOS, CP/M, etc. A couple different companies produce x86 processors, but the bulk of them are produced by Intel. It is expected that this processor will eventually be completely replaced by the Merced, but the Merced development schedule is somewhat behind. Also, it should be noted that the Pentium III processor has stirred some controversy by including a "fingerprint" that will enable individual computer usage of web pages etc. to be accurately tracked.
**XBL**
An XML Binding Language document is used to associate executable content with an XML tag. It is itself an XML file, and is used most frequently (although not exclusively) in conjunction with XUL.
**XHTML**
The Extensible Hypertext Mark-up Language is essentially a cleaner, stricter version of HTML. It is a proper subset of XML.
**XML**
The Extensible Mark-up Language is a subset of SGML and a superset of XHTML. It is used for numerous things including (among many others) RSS and RDF.
**XML-RPC**
XML-RPC provides a fairly lightweight means by which one computer can execute a program on a co-operating machine across a network like the Internet. It is based on XML and is used for everything from fetching stock quotes to checking weather forcasts.
**XO**
The energy-efficient, kid-friendly laptop produced by the OLPC project. It runs Sugar for its window manager and Linux for its OS. It sports numerous built-in features like wireless networking, a video camera & microphone, a few USB ports, and audio in/out jacks. It comes with several educational applications (which it refers to as "Activities"), most of which are written in Python.
**XSL**
The Extensible Stylesheet Language is like CSS for XML. It provides a means of describing how an XML resource should be displayed.
**XSLT**
XSL Transformations are used to transform one type of XML into another. It is a component of XSL that can be (and often is) used independently.
**XUL**
An XML User-Interface Language document is used to define a user interface for an application

using XML to specify the individual controls as well as the overall layout.

**Y2K**

The general class of problems resulting from the wrapping of computers' internal date timers is given this label in honor of the most obvious occurrence -- when the year changes from 1999 to 2000 (abbreviated in some programs as 99 to 00 indicating a backwards time movement). Contrary to popular belief, these problems will not all manifest themselves on the first day of 2000, but will in fact happen over a range of dates extending out beyond 2075. A computer that does not have problems prior to the beginning of 2001 is considered "Y2K compliant", and a computer that does not have problems within the next ten years or so is considered for all practical purposes to be "Y2K clean". Whether or not a given computer is "clean" depends upon both its OS and its applications (and in some unfortunate cases, its hardware). The quick rundown on common home / small business machines (roughly from best to worst) is that:

- All Mac OS systems are okay until at least the year 2040. By that time a patch should be available.
- All BeOS systems are okay until the year 2040 (2038?). By that time a patch should be available.
- Most UNIX versions are either okay or currently have free fixes available (and typically would not have major problems until 2038 or later in any case).
- NewtonOS has a problem with the year 2010, but has a free fix available.
- Newer AmigaOS systems are okay; older ones have a problem with the year 2000 but have a free fix available. They also have a year 2077 problem that does not yet have a free fix.
- Some OS/2 systems have a year 2000 problem, but free fixes are available.
- All CP/M versions have a year 2000 problem, but free fixes are available.
- PC-DOS has a year 2000 problem, but a free fix is available.
- DR-DOS has a year 2000 problem, but a free fix is available.
- Different versions of GEOS have different problems ranging from minor year 2000 problems (with fixes in the works) to larger year 2080 problems (that do not have fixes yet). The only problem that may not have a fix in time is the year 2000 problem on the Apple ][ version of GEOS; not only was that version discontinued, unlike the other GEOS versions it no longer has a parent company to take care of it.
- All MS-Windows versions (except possibly Windows 2000 and Windows ME) have multiple problems with the year 2000 and/or 2001, most of which have free fixes but some of which still lack free fixes as of this writing. Even new machines off the shelf that are labelled "Y2K Compliant" usually are not unless additional software is purchased and installed. Basically WinNT and WinCE can be properly patched, Windows '98 can be patched to work properly through 2000 (possibly not 2001), Windows '95 can be at least partially patched for 2000 (but not 2001) but is not being guaranteed by Microsoft, and Windows 3.1 cannot be fully patched.
- MS-DOS has problems with at least the year 2000 (and probably more). None of its problems have been addressed as of this writing. Possible fixes are to change over to either PC-DOS or DR-DOS.

Results vary wildly for common applications, so it is better to be safe than sorry and check out the ones that you use. It should also be noted that some of the biggest expected Y2K problems will be at the two ends of the computer spectrum with older legacy mainframes (such as power some large banks) and some of the various tiny embedded computers (such as power most burgler alarms and many assorted appliances). Finally, it should also be mentioned that some older WinTel boxes and Amigas may have Y2K problems in their hardware requiring a card addition or replacement.

**Z-Machine**

A virtual machine optimized for running interactive fiction, interactive tutorials, and other interactive things of a primarily textual nature. Z-Machines have been ported to almost every platform in use today. Z-machine bytecode is usually called Z-code. The Glulx virtual machine is of the same idea but somewhat more modern in concept.

**Z80**

The Z80 series of processors is a CISC design and is not being used in too many new stand-alone computer systems, but can still be occasionally found in embedded systems. It is the most popular processor for CP/M machines.

**Zaurus**

The Zaurus is a brand of PDA. It is generally in between a Palm and a Newton in capability.

**zip**

There are three common zips in the computer world that are completely different from one another. One is a type of removable removable disk slightly larger (physically) and vastly larger (capacity) than a floppy. The second is a group of programs used for running interactive fiction. The third is a group of programs used for compression.

**Zoomer**

The Zoomer is a type of PDA. Zoomers all use GEOS for their OS and are / were produced by numerous different companies and are thus found under numerous different names. The "classic" Zoomers are known as the Z-7000, the Z-PDA, and the GRiDpad and were made by Casio, Tandy, and AST respectively. Newer Zoomers include HP's OmniGo models, Hyundai's Gulliver (which may not have actually been released to the general public), and Nokia's Communicator line of PDA / cell phone hybrids.

www.ingramcontent.com/pod-product-compliance
Lightning Source LLC
Chambersburg PA
CBHW081810300426
44116CB00014B/2300